AF316635

PRAISE FOR WHAT REMAINS IS LOVE

"This love story between brother and sister is one too often missing from family accounts. It challenges the artificial division of gender, and unrealized love."

–Gloria Steinem, writer, feminist activist, organizer, leader

"What remains besides love in this testament is the mysterious and awesome resilience of the human psyche."

–James B. Nicola, author of Playing the Audience, Wind in the Cave, Natural Tendencies, and many more

"A moving and courageous account of a journey toward healing. DiMauro's grief becomes a transformative, restorative force with the power to generate more love. An incredible accomplishment!"

–Madalina Blanton, Reiki Master/Teacher/Wellness Facilitator, soultoearthhealing.com

"What Remains Is Love teaches how to be in your grief process with awareness, self-love, and grace."

–Elizabeth Cohen, Ph.D. Clinical Psychologist, Author, Director of the Center for CBT in New York City

"DiMauro writes with equal honesty about the complexities of family and how love, duty, and grief intertwine as each member struggles to find their own way through."

–Erin Walker, Ph.D., Licensed Clinical Psychologist, New York City

"Weaving together family stories, inner dialogue, and spiritual insight, DiMauro has given us a poignant and loving account of loss and grief."

–Peeka Trenkle, M.Div., Creator of the Green Medicine program, New York Open Center, peekatrenkle.com

"What Remains Is Love is a searing and poignant account of the physical and emotional toll of grief."

–Virginia-Lee Webb, Ph.D., AAA.VL.Webb Consultants, Arts of Africa and Oceania, LLC

WHAT REMAINS IS LOVE

My Journey of Losing My Brother and Healing through Grief

JOANNE DIMAURO

COBSCOOK BAY PRESS

Melancolie, a sculpture by Albert György*

This is what grief is.
A hole ripped through the very fabric of your being.
The hole eventually heals along the jagged edges that remain.
It may even shrink in size.
But that hole will always be there.
A piece of you always missing.
For where there is deep grief, there was great love.
Don't be ashamed of your grief.
Don't judge it.
Don't suppress it.
Don't rush it.
Rather, acknowledge it.
Lean into it.
Listen to it.
Feel it.
Sit with it.
Sit with the pain.
And remember the love.
This is where the healing will begin.

– Monica Bobbitt

(This heartbreakingly beautiful sculpture, Melancolie, created by Albert György (living in Switzerland, but born in Romania) can be found in Geneva in a small park on the promenade (Quai du Mont Blanc) along the shore of Lake Geneva.)

TABLE OF CONTENTS

INTRODUCTION

This is my grief journey through the memories of my beloved brother and our relationship. It's a story about family, about death and dying, about coming to terms with loss—and my personal navigation of grief throughout his illness and untimely death. It has been a profound learning process for me and my family. My wish for the reader is to illuminate the fear around death and dying, to discover what lies beneath it, and what it can teach us about embracing both the bond and the loss. My hope is that my journey through love, laughter, life, trauma, dying, death, culture and the perpetual connection with those we've lost might support and enlighten other seekers on their own voyage.

Above all, my story is a testament of love—dedicated to my brother Jon, and shared with anyone who's ever wondered: How do I survive this?

You're not alone.

A NOTE TO THE READER

Grief can be messy, mystifying, overwhelming and chaotic. And not linear. Just when I think I've healed a painful wound, old memories or feelings cycle back and flood my consciousness, haltingly, sometimes gradually, and in no particular order, reminding me of a past joy or painful occurrence, waiting below the surface for an opportunity to emerge again. Since joy and pain are flipsides of the same coin, it is important for me to share my memories in order to heal, for the healing happens in connecting with you, the reader, and in being witnessed.

And healing is arduous—it dictates its own course. I hope my journey through grief inspires you to embrace your own healing process, giving you the space and freedom to honor your emotional experience.

Me and my brother Jon, 1962

This book is dedicated to:

My brother Jon, the peaceful warrior,
who always took the road less traveled
and inspired us all.

You are loved and missed every day.

I

BIRDS AS MESSENGERS

September 11, 2022

Today is September 11th. Another innocent blue sky and delicious Indian summer weather, unsuspecting and reminiscent of what was to come that fateful day twenty-one years ago.

Two profound tragedies in my life are: 1) the collective loss of the attack on the Twin Towers on September 11th, 2001, and 2) the personal loss of the death of my brother; both scarring my heart permanently.

My brother Jon died 11 days ago at age 62. He lived for 46 months with brain cancer. I have a recently formed wound on my heart, a lesion that keeps bleeding. People say the pain of losing a child is incomparable. I have no children, but Jon was my kid brother. Losing him feels like losing my child. I took care of him a great deal when we were young and our connection is special.

My brother keeps visiting me. I was unaware of his death the morning he died and didn't find out until much later that day. My friend Miranda said, "it will happen when you least expect it and you'll get the word." It happened that way with her mother. She was right. I had taken my energetic eyes off Jon temporarily, and he slipped out the back door without me knowing it. He passed away at 2:37 a.m. but I didn't find out until after 5 pm.

That morning, I was running a little late, so I did an abbreviated version of my usual morning meditation and prayer ritual out on my terrace. Surprisingly a FLOCK of pigeons flew to my terrace and rested briefly on the window ledge. More often, one, maybe two will settle and perch and I'd get a bit of sadistic pleasure blasting them away with my high-powered water gun, but today it was like an alarming scene out of the movie "The Birds." I left them alone but did note how abnormal that was and hurried on to my day.

I have a geranium plant I placed on my terrace I call my "Jon" plant. I've had it for the duration of his illness on the altar I created for him on the bedroom windowsill. It had grown, thrived and blossomed so much that I moved it outside to my terrace and tied it to the railings to keep it upright. Within the last few months before his death, it started to wither and droop gauntly so about a month before he died, although hesitant to do so for fear it would jinx things, I told myself I would accept his current health situation and decided to trim it back.

They say birds are messengers of the spirit. Jon LOVED birds. He would sit for hours in his chair at the kitchen table watching them pecking at the feeders, outside the window. He knew all birds and could imitate their calls and did so, often, delighting us.

The morning of his death, after the strange incident with the flock of pigeons visiting me, I looked down at my Jon plant and saw a white leaf blossoming at the top of the plant. And below pressed close to it on the deck floor, were two tiny white feathers. I believe that was Jon flying by on his way up to soul world, waving goodbye, letting me know he got his wings.

(my Jon plant)

August 27th, 2022, I was painstakingly waiting for word
of when/if Jon had passed. The last day I saw him was on August
13th. He wanted to be left alone with Lisa, his wife, and requested
no more contact with us. We were to be notified after his death,
by Lisa through an email, with no other communication in the
interim. Those were his wishes, which my family and I found so
difficult to accept and respect. We were always a tight-knit family,
albeit dysfunctional.

I was distraught with anticipatory anxiety and grief, so my
husband Bruno and I drove to Sea Girt Beach for some sanity
and soul healing. Once there, I placed our blanket and bags down
on the sand, kicked off my sandals and walked down to the water
and dipped into the ocean. This is the most healing thing I do for
myself. It was a glorious, perfect beach day. In my mind, I was with
Jon in the water. He loved the ocean as much as I did and I have
many memories of us at the beach, swimming, laughing and body
surfing in the sea together throughout the years, as kids growing
up in Maine, as adults at the shore, on a sailing trip snorkeling off
our boat in the Caribbean Sea. My memories are abundant.

Spending time together that day in the ocean, frolicking
in the waves, just reveling in the glory of the sea was a blessing. I
stood at the shoreline saying prayers for my brother and praying

to him, asking for a sign from him, from someone, to let me know he's okay, that he's being comforted and attended to. I was desperate. *Please, anything, any sign to reassure me.*

When I walked back up to the blanket, I noticed a small white feather stuck to the Velcro on my sandal. Jon, or his guardian angel, came to tell me he was safe—not to worry. Enormous relief washed over me, temporarily easing my mind. I wanted to believe this was a message. That he was tranquil, free of pain, content and being cared for.

This was the exact time he was moved to the Gosnell Hospice House close by him, placed in the loving care of those beautiful helpers in that sacred space.

Jon sends me messages all the time through birds. A feather will drop at my feet unexpectedly when I feel myself slipping into a pit of grief and despair again. When I need reassurance from him that he's doing okay now. That he's in a better place. *"Thank you for these signs, Gianni,* (our endearing nickname for Jon). *I hope we continue to communicate, and I will be on the lookout for more messages from you."*

September 21, 2022

I had a dream about Jon last night. He was healthy but seemed quiet. Forlorn. His hair was long and pulled back in a ponytail like he wore it in the 80's. And he was fully healed, standing upright talking to me. He asked me for the name of the two Homeopathic and Herbal remedies I had suggested he take for his illness. I responded and he said he was healthy and fine, no signs of cancer, but he wanted to continue to take those two remedies as a precautionary measure. They wouldn't be too expensive. I suggested he also take a good multivitamin which would cost more. He agreed to that. I woke up feeling apprehensive. *"Jon, are you ok? Are you in a good place now physically, mentally, emotionally? I hope and pray that you are."*

2

LIVING IN THE WINDOWS
BETWEEN THE PARENTHESES

We're having a Memorial mass for Jon at St. Peter's Church this morning followed by a gathering for friends and family at cousin Jody's house. *"I know you didn't want any funeral or service, and you always said no one ever listens to you. I'm listening to you, but you know your mother…She feels the need to "send you off" with a Catholic service. I was looking for some kind of message from you to let me know how you feel about it. Jon, are you okay with this?"*

A memory popped into my mind during meditation of when we were kids; we'd be sitting in church right after communion and Jon would act out some ridiculous antics of pretending to scrape the stuck host from the roof of his mouth. He'd have me in silent stitches, so much so, that I couldn't look at him without bursting into laughter. My mother would have to separate us in the pew. I'm interpreting this as a sign that he's okay with the service today. And he will be there keeping it light. Also, there was a statue of a bird at the podium: another positive sign from him as well.

After the mass we want to be with friends and family to celebrate him. I made a slide show. *I hope you like it. We ordered your favorite cream rolls. Remember when Dad would go to work at his night job at Spector Trucking Company and on his way back, he'd bring home day-old pastries from Cushman's bakery? Your favorite were the cream rolls. We'd be lying in bed saying our good nights to Dad as he was leaving and I can still hear your little voice, "don't forget the creams!"*

"Living in the windows between the parentheses" is the term I use to describe the time during those 46 months of my brother's illness where I felt I could take a deep breath and relax a bit in the temporary relief of a "good" medical report or a "good" MRI. We all reveled in those pretend pauses during his illness. We were hopeful. Maybe all our prayers, the energy healing he was receiving and his due diligence in maintaining a strict diet was helping him. His daily commitment to wearing the Optune device on his head, like a warrior's helmet, a shield which was supposed to protect him from cancer regrowth; maybe it was all working to heal him. Even though that cranial contraption he wore 24/7 was awkward, painful, uncomfortable and cumbersome, and drew inquisitive stares and unwanted attention from people, he accepted it and persevered.

Maybe all the conventional and alternative therapies he was using and his constant commitment to maintaining a positive outlook and lightness of spirit were making a difference. The love and support from Lisa, his devoted wife, and from his extensive team of medical personnel and healers. And from all the outpouring of love from family members, friends, "Prayer Warriors" who didn't even know Jon, and spirit guides from beyond this realm. I specifically got Reiki trained and certified to be able to send him distance energy for the highest possible healing for whatever was needed most for him in the moment, and I sent it to him often. Perhaps all these ingredients were helping to heal him and extend his life.

Jon was connected to a higher source, more so than most of us. In meditation, some of us may have the ability to sense or see a spirit guide which we can call on to help us in times of need. In meditation, Jon said he saw stadiums of people supporting him. I guess he was popular there. When he told me this, I wanted to believe they were cheering him on and he was receiving healing energy from beyond this worldly realm. I was hopeful.

But perhaps they wanted him there and were calling him. Maybe they needed him more than we did.

In the windows between the parentheses I could decompress, briefly, from worry and fear. Really be present in the glory and gratitude of the day. Noticing the deep blueness of the sky. I could step into moments of carefree enjoyment in my life, maybe even consider making some plans for the near future. Possibly taking a trip or planning when I come to Maine in the summer, how I could get Jon to the beach; how, somehow, I could take him swimming in the ocean. Fantasizing about little excursions we could do together with him. Maybe even rent a place at the Jersey shore and he and Lisa could come down for a week. Or take a trip with them to Florida in the winter. Things like that. Positive possible occurrences before the next upcoming test or scan, or a report of Jon having a "bad" day triggered immediate concerns and worries into the crevices of my mind, gradually diminishing positivity and hope and replacing it with fear. And my faith would puncture and deflate.

Grief is erratic. Illusive. Strange. We're afraid of it; of death and dying, of endings. *I'm* afraid of grief. The experts say to dip your toe in, and then take it out. And dip it in again and come out. I'm afraid if I dip my toe in, I'll get pulled under by the riptide and be swept away in a tsunami. So, I avoid it until my feelings pile up and then the dam bursts.

But then I feel better. I notice when I allow my grief to be expressed, the joys in my life are much more ebullient. I find myself laughing gleefully and screaming out loud playing tennis and enjoying the sun and the leaves and the wind. Maybe this is life's trick: Live loud—full out. The Buddhists teach moderation and balance; how it's mindful to maintain that mid-range of emotions; not too high and not too low. But I'm playing with the extremes right now. I want to have my grief and not be afraid of it.

Everyone handles grief differently. Some people need to clean up and clear out the deceased person's belongings right away. Lisa is doing that. Jon was quite the hoarder and literally kept EVERYTHING. I would have liked to have been participatory in sifting through his personal items, touching his things and his clothes; reminiscing, in the particular scent of him, but I was not given that opportunity. Lisa didn't want to share that; she wanted to keep that ritual personal.

I'm learning I'm not like that. I'm in no hurry to let Jon go. I'm pleased when I open up Amazon Prime on the TV and see his name under "Who's watching?" since I added him to my Prime account long ago so he could watch movies. I'm comforted seeing all his pictures on my altar and talisman for healing and cards and prayer books for him. I'm not ready to depart from all that yet.

Jon was an empath and a highly sensitive person. He listened to you with his whole being and couldn't tune anything out. He had no protective filter the way most of us have.

He used to say to me, "Just put your Teflon shit suit on, Joanne. When she talks to you, let it hit you and then let it roll right off you." He might have been trying to convince himself of that technique but he couldn't quite master it.

Some of Jon's "truisms" were: *Life's too short. Don't let anyone steal your peace. Control your mind, control your world.* He was a peaceful warrior and advocated these truisms his entire life. But because he was empathic and sensitive, and downright controlling at times, he couldn't help himself trying to fix and save everyone. He listened too much.

Reminds me of a lightworker, Eva Perrokos. She was an empath and a healer and yet she died of cancer. Maybe she absorbed everyone else's pain and problems, their grief and misery like a sponge, and her physical body became a toxic receptacle for it all. Like the book cover states, *The Body Keeps the Score*. Maybe she listened too much too.

3
MORE TIME

I wake up at one a.m. with a restless disturbed feeling. Technically I should be "in the window" now but I'm not. My grief is deep. Not right on the surface anymore but thoughts and feelings that seemingly come up out of nowhere and feel like a vice grip clamping on my heart.

"Are you okay Jon? What's going on with you now? Are you enjoying life in spirit? Golfing, laughing it up and eating at all-you-can-eat buffets with Dad? I know how much you both loved those places." Or are these just stories I tell myself so I can feel some sense of comfort and ease and live in the window of my life here? *"Are you completely healed in body and mind?"* Silly thoughts too, like, *"what are you wearing?"*

One of the last times I spent with Jon alone was in the beginning of June 2022. I was giving Lisa a caregiver's break so she could get away for a few days and recharge. He wasn't wearing the Optune device anymore and had given up his strict diet since the doctors had said both were failing to keep his cancer at bay. He was eating everything now, giving himself this one last enjoyment—the pleasure of food. Jon loved food.

The new protocol was, every two weeks, he would receive
an IV infusion of the immunotherapy drug Keytruda or Avastin.
I don't remember which one. He had tried them both. This was
supposed to give him more time…

More time. What is this *more time* concept? Stephen
Jenkinson, renowned activist, international teacher, author,
palliative care expert (known as the "Griefwalker"), says in all his
years of working with the dying, this tends to be the one thing we
all want at the end.

But more time for what? More time to die? To struggle in
pain, without the use of his right arm; to live in this handicapped
depleted state, a mere shadow of his former athletic self? Days
filled with endless doctors' visits and treatments and knowing he
has a terminal illness with no cure? He was ALWAYS exhausted
now. Every day was a struggle to just get out of bed and walk to
the kitchen table. He was angry and frustrated and depressed.
Who wouldn't be. And yet he fought it, persevered, reset himself
constantly and wanted "more time" and always said he was grateful
for another day to be alive.

I'm not so sure I would have my brother's tenacity of spirit.
But then again when it's my time I might balk and be kicking
and screaming, "wait! not yet!" James Fries, MD, professor of
medicine at Stamford University School of Medicine, talks about
compression of morbidity, his term for what we all aim for at the
end of our lives. Basically, it's living – healthy, healthy, healthy and
then we die. Unfortunately, we don't have control of the outcome.
More often than not, it's not that clean. Dying is messy.

…When we went in for Jon's IV infusion treatment, it was
a premature summer day, unusually beautiful weather for this
time of year in Maine. He loved driving and was still driving then.
Thank God because he couldn't stand my driving.

I pushed him in the wheelchair from the car into the facility
and sat next to him in the cancer ward while he got connected

to the IV. He was talking a mile a minute to the nurse, which I realized was his way when he got scared and nervous. I tried to remain nonchalant but it made ME nervous when he talked so much. I was afraid the nurse wouldn't be able to concentrate and would insert the tube incorrectly.

Once it was set though, she offered us a selection of snacks to choose from which Jon enthusiastically ordered and urged me to get some too. He appreciated and took advantage of all the "amenities" the place offered. We chatted easily, randomly, and then he closed his eyes and we both got quiet while he rested. *"Were you visualizing your spirit guides sending you healing energy through that IV?"*

When Jon was done with the infusion, he seemed to have a second wind, so I suggested we go for some seasonal summer foods at our old stomping grounds, starting off with clam cakes at Ken's Place for lunch. Then he drove us to Old Orchard Beach for their famous Pier Fries and we sat at the end of a side street in the car, eating them, looking out at the ocean. I got out of the car and went down to the water's edge to put my toes in. He could still drive, but he couldn't walk very far at all now, he didn't have the strength or the energy it took to walk, so he stayed in the car. On my walk back from the shore, I had spotted a bench that was on the beach sand, but not too far from the car. I was hoping he could get out of the car and walk to it. Sit on the beach. I mentioned it but could tell he didn't feel up for it so I didn't push him.

Then on the drive back home we stopped at Ken's Place again for fried clams this time. I went in to order the food and left him outside in the car because, as he would say, jokingly, he was *"co-voiding"* people. COVID was surging. I came back to the car, to wait outside with him for our order to be called over the loudspeaker. He had gotten out of the car, was standing, leaning up against it, enjoying the sun and watching some antique cars driving by. He had a fondness for cars and made comments about each one to me.

…Jon loved his Matchbox cars and over the years, amassed quite an extensive collection. As kids, we'd sit in his bedroom, he'd take down the cases off the shelf, where they were meticulously stored, and we'd play with them, competing for "first pick" to select our favorites. The sports cars would go first. My favorite was a yellow Ferrari…

Together that day, we ate all our favorite Maine summer foods. *"Did we even have an ice cream at Bayley's as well? I don't recall. Remember years ago, when Beal's Ice Cream was the only real homemade ice cream place around and we'd drive all the way out to Gorham just to get some?"*

This day was special. Memorable. Just Jon and me. Relaxed and easy. I believed the immunotherapy drug was working. I think he did too. It was.

And then it wasn't anymore.

Jon doing what he loved – driving.   *Jon and his wife Lisa, summer 2022*

4

GRIEF, GUILT, MEMORIES & REGRETS

October 15, 2022

A sparrow landed on the terrace on my Jon plant. So unusual. I'm on the 10th floor, and other than pigeons, birds never come up here. It was a beautiful day, and I had the door propped open. I didn't see him but heard him first; a bird song, and so I tentatively stepped closer to the door not wanting to scare him away but to see and watch him. He sang me a little song and then flew off. *"I believe it was you Jon stopping by for a quick visit to say hello and wish me a Happy Anniversary."*

Jon was light energy. He had an aura, a presence that was palpable and lit up a room. Everyone was attracted to him.

When I attended the program at the Institute for Integrative Nutrition, we were on a short break at the Lincoln Jazz Center. One wall was ceiling to floor clear glass and the sun was shining. We had been inside in the dark auditorium, all 1200 of us students, with no natural lighting, so once we were let out on a break, everyone gravitated towards the windows, towards the light. We are all just plants needing and wanting the sun for nourishment. Jon was nourishment for the soul. People recognized the light within him and gravitated to that. We all did.

November 18, 2022

I wake up with a foreboding sense that something's not right.

I realize what's wrong is that Jon's not here anymore. I'm missing his presence on earth, and a wave of grief overtakes me and I'm drowning in it again. I cry and Bruno rubs my back as I let my sobs and tears go. It's just love that's wrenching inside me. Love for Jon. I think about him and relive some of the good times and some sad memories, toss and turn around for a while, and then settle down and fall back to sleep. That's grief announcing its presence.

November 27, 2022

It's Thanksgiving week and the days leading up to the holidays have me struggling with sadness, missing and remembering Jon. Fun times, difficult times with the family. It's all a stirring of raucous emotions. I'm crying a lot and feeling unsociable. I force myself to participate in activities with Bruno's family —Thanksgiving dinner. I'm okay until I talk about Jon then I start to break down. I sense people feeling uncomfortable and they change the subject. No one asks me how I'm doing except my sister-in-law Vilma. It's as if it never happened or they don't want to upset me and shroud the levity of the holiday party.

It's awkward or scary for us to talk about death because we're grief illiterate. It's a natural part of life but not a pleasant topic.

We humans are strange. Most of the time, we're walking around preoccupied; alone, in our heads, self-absorbed in "stinkin thinkin." I can attest to being guilty of that. I used to believe it was because I was insecure and shy. A therapist offered a different perspective: shyness might be the flip side of a big ego. Hmm… a liberating concept. She may be right. We assume everyone is looking, evaluating or judging our manner of speaking and acting, when in fact, they might take notice momentarily, before resuming focus on the priority of their lives.

Jon wasn't shy at all. He was loyal to his authenticity in any situation. Completely comfortable in his own skin, he always shared with humor, intelligence, and a deep sensitivity and yet could be fully engaged and interested in mundane conversation and everyday minutiae. I admired that about him, and he inspires me to be real; to be in my truth. At his 40th birthday party I raised my glass in a toast to him: "Don't ever change Jon. Stay just the way you are."

*Nephew Ryan and brothers, Jon and Joe,
at Jon's 40th Birthday party*

One night, years ago, when we siblings were sitting around sharing dating escapades, Jon told my sister Jan and me about a woman he had met (they went out, maybe a few times), and she asked him to be her New Year's Eve date at a fancy function at the Eastland Hotel. Weeks had passed and he tried calling her to get the specifics about the event, but she wasn't returning any of his calls. So, he just showed up at the Eastland Ballroom the night of the event and waited out front for her. She arrived with another date, obviously shocked and appalled that Jon was there.

Jon acted like nothing was out of the ordinary, was his usual friendly self, walked in with them, sat with her and her date and enjoyed himself, making conversation with everyone at the table. He told us he didn't mind yet refused to let her off the hook for not being honest. For not notifying him their date was cancelled.

If that had been me, I would have been ashamed and humiliated. He said it didn't bother him at all.

I'm not so sure I believed him.

He and his wife Lisa had a unique relationship. They didn't live together. She spent most of her time upstate taking care of her mother and working in her art studio there, and he was living down state in Portland, in their house. He said he enjoyed his life as a "married bachelor;" that he had the best of both worlds. He always came alone to most family holiday gatherings and events, making excuses for Lisa's absences. We were concerned but didn't pry. He was covering for her, most likely. Alcohol would be flowing at these parties and it could be triggering for Lisa. (I understand it now —it can affect me in that way too.)

Usually, the initial topic someone brings up reflects their immediate thoughts—of what's most important to them. The day after Jon's brain surgery, I went to the hospital to see him and as I walked into his room the first words out of his mouth, to me, were, "Guess what...Lisa's coming home!"

November 29, 2022

I've been discriminating lately; muzzling and sharing my feelings of grief only with those individuals I trust who make me feel safe. My grief is more manageable when I do express it. Maybe because I'm releasing it by sharing it or it's just that time has passed. It's been almost three months since Jon died. I had a thought this morning, ... *Jon, maybe your spirit has left this realm and you're completely in another world now. Does it take that long to "leave?"*

Maybe that's why I feel lighter and his presence is not so visceral? I'm not sure if I feel happy or sad about this. I should feel relieved that he is completely transitioned and has no need or attachments to anything or anyone of this world. I should feel good about that and let him go and focus on my life. I know he would want me to. *Go and live your life!* He would always say. I'm trying to let go of the "shoulds" but it's hard. I envy him and where he might be now.

...As kids, he and I would get into these jags of playing board games over Christmas school break or February vacation. One year it was Chinese checkers. I can recall mornings when I'd open my eyes and he'd be standing by my bed with the Chinese checkerboard all set up just waiting for me to wake up. I'd immediately sit up in bed, and we'd start playing right then and there on my bed. We loved games and our passion for them continued as we grew older.

I'm currently addicted to a word play app on my phone. Always late to the technology game, I regret not getting on this sooner so I could have introduced it to Jon. He would have loved it. Even as a twelve-year-old he was a wordsmith. My sister Jan was dating two guys at the same time, Michael Mezerschmidt and Michael Beckwith. Jon would say to her, "Don't mess around with Mezerschmidt" and "to heck with Beckwith."

He enjoyed doing the daily jumbles and crosswords and we liked playing Boggle but since he lost the use of his right arm from the effects of the brain tumor and could only operate with his left, this word play app would have been ideal for him. When he got sick initially, we were all sending him word game books, unaware of how difficult this would be for him with his one arm handicap.

We take so much for granted until we lose it.

Jon and I share our love for Scrabble. In the early stages of his illness, when I would come and stay with him to take over caregiving for Lisa, we'd play Scrabble daily for HOURS at a time, using nine letters and cross referencing the dictionary, creating all kinds of words. Words we couldn't even define. I know it was cheating and we were establishing our own rules for Scrabble. He'd always win though. He's much smarter than me.

I'm sorry, Jon; I pushed you to play that long and hard.

I now know how tiring and challenging that must have been on his brain. We'd have music playing in the background too. It must have been tedious and taxing for him, but he never complained and he was a good sport about it all. He tolerated my insistence on playing with nine letters and keeping score.

Later, as his disease progressed, he asked me if we could use seven letters to play and not keep score. I didn't turn the music on anymore either.

I get a pit in my stomach when I think about how I pushed him with my desire and MY need to make him better and to try and heal him. All those days when we would meet over FaceTime for physical therapy sessions and I would work him to fatigue. What a blessing that I'd made a career of it and could work with him, and I'd rearrange my schedule and make myself available for whenever he needed and wanted a session. I had built up my own business in the field over the last twenty years, had a stable of consistent clientele, so at this point, was able to easily shift my appointments around and make Jon my priority client.

It was a great excuse for me to be with him every week and monitor him. We'd talk and check in, and depending upon his mood and energy level that day, I'd instruct him on rehab exercises, and we'd have some laughs and some intimate sharing time too.

I loved those sessions. I'd coach him and he would diligently do the best he could with the exercises. "Push push push... and, right back down," he'd jokingly mock me with my repetitive cues. Often when I'm in session with a client now, I smile to myself, still hearing his voice.

But I was in my own denial of how ill he really was. *I KNOW he can get well. I know we can do it,* I'd think to myself. I couldn't face the truth nor accept the situation and his diagnosis. I desperately wanted to fix him and make it all better. I'd wake up in the middle of the night brainstorming about different exercises we could do to get his hand, his mobility and his strength back, what tools and equipment I could order for him that would help him in this process. I needed to explore all options for recovery, leaving no stone unturned. HE wanted to believe he could rehabilitate completely and he wanted to make ME feel better by going along with everything I suggested, pushing himself to exhaustion. Denial was our coping mechanism.

It was difficult and painful for me to see his atrophied right arm hanging listlessly from his subluxated shoulder like a dead branch of a tree, attached to the trunk but weakly holding on. I remember that day when he was still going out to a rehab center and I went with him and questioned his physical therapist on how we could address this. Wasn't it dangerous letting his arm hang like that? Shouldn't he keep it supported in an arm sling? But it was just another handicap on the endless list of things with which he coped. He had so many other issues to address and this was a low priority. But I was concerned.

Years ago, I had hand surgery and needed a nerve block. I woke up after surgery with no feeling in my right arm, terrified until the block wore off and I could regain sensation. I can't imagine how frightening it must have been for Jon knowing that he would never get the full use of his right limb back.

I left him that day. I had to catch the bus back to New York City and Lisa hadn't arrived back home yet. I was angry at her for that and was anxious about leaving him alone, having to fend for himself, but he insisted he would be fine. I left him sitting in his spot at the kitchen table, in a makeshift sling, looking helpless and forlorn, with that crazy Optune device on his head, scrolling through his iPad, my eyes staving off tears. I knew he wouldn't be able to stand seeing me having any pity or concern for his suffering. It was too painful for him. He had said if the situation were reversed and I was the sick one, he wouldn't be able to be around me.

As soon as I got on the bus, I started researching on my phone for a better arm sling and would certainly reach out to Lisa to discuss this.

For the past two years, I couldn't "stomach" his illness anymore, couldn't "swallow" it. He was the one with brain cancer, but I was sick right along with him with severe abdominal pains and digestive problems. I couldn't detach. My co-dependency was too strong.

I felt like Woody Allen's character in the movie "Zelig," morphing into the people who surrounded him, like growing side curls while in the company of Hasidic Jews.

And with every physical functionality I had at my disposal came the inevitable realization that any of it would be difficult for Jon. Everyday mundane things. I was obsessed with my thinking. *"Jon can't do this anymore,"* I'd think while standing on one leg in the shower, scrubbing the sole of my foot with a washcloth. Crazy stuff too. I'd imagine taking him with me on the back of my bike as I rode down the Hudson River Park, lost in a fantasy of him gleefully enjoying this as much as I, and I'd have a momentary window of relief, a haven from my mental torture.

When I'd walk on the sand at the beach, I'd think, *"Jon couldn't do this. He wouldn't be able to balance."* And then I'd be brainstorming on how I could make it work for him. I spotted a beach wheelchair with huge wheels at Sea Girt Beach and sent a picture of it to Lisa in hopes that she could investigate and find out if they offered one at their local beach. She did and they did.

My brother got to use it twice in his last summer.

And while he was committed to that strict Ketogenic diet for 3 ½ years, I'd research foods that he could eat and I'd order him special snacks and breads and treats that would give his diet some variety, something to anticipate. Something special to break up the monotony.

On one level, it was a relief when the doctors said the diet wasn't helping to keep his cancer from spreading anymore. He embraced eating everything then.

"I may as well die fat and happy, what difference does it make," he'd say, since he enjoyed eating and it was one of his last few pleasures. We brought him all the foods he loved, and his eyes widened when the desserts were set out.

"Snacks and sweets on the days that begin with S," suggests Michael Pollan in his book *Food Rules*. Jon extended it to, "snacks and sweets on the days that end in Y."

He always loved sweets. We have that in common. As a youngster, he'd drag the step stool over to the kitchen cabinets and climb up onto the countertop to reach for the marshmallow fluff, find a spoon in the drawer to scoop it out and eat from the jar. I have a picture of him in his little footy pajamas caught in the act.

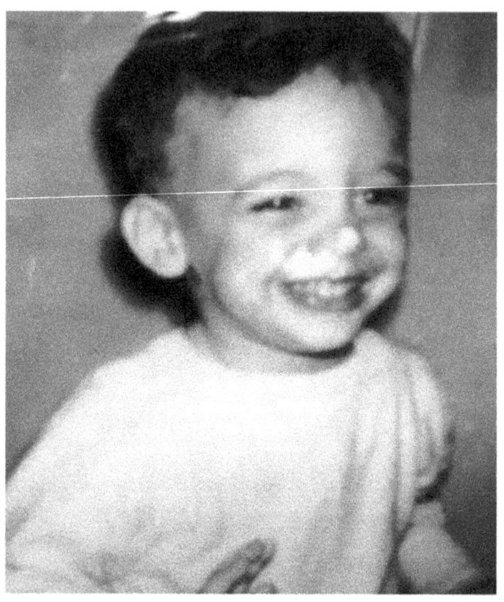

Marshmallow Fluff face Jon

He loved to talk about food and would describe, in detail, all that was offered at various all-you-can-eat buffets around town; ones that Dad and he often frequented in the past. There is one here in Koreatown that runs a city block long. I wish he was still here and I could take him there.

5

A DARK TRUTH DAWNS

It'd been months since I'd seen him, and after the long bus ride up to Maine from New York City, I was looking forward to spending some quality time with him. I'd creep in the back door, tiptoe to his bedside with the intention of giving him a gentle hug hello, so as not to be jarring, but he'd dismiss my attention and immediately start barking out orders.

"Go get yourself something to eat. There're leftovers in the fridge or make yourself a sandwich. Go on," he'd say, running down a list of what was in the kitchen.

I'd think to myself, *"well it's nice to see you too, Jon."* But then I'd realize it was his way of deflecting his uncomfortability with the intimacy. His way of hiding so I wouldn't be sad or shocked with the declining state of his health.

So, I'd act nonchalant too, as if I'd just seen him yesterday, and I'd talk about something benign like the bus ride up, to allow us both time to settle into being together again.

One of the first occasions I drove him to an appointment, he insisted on walking from the car into the medical center, most likely wanting to prove his capability to himself and to his doctor.

After his appointment, I went outside ahead of him to get the car from the parking lot, drove it up to the front door of the facility so he wouldn't have to walk as far, but, rather than parking it so he had easy access to the passenger door, I absently parked the car in the opposite direction, forcing him to walk farther around.

I happened to glance in the rearview mirror, guilt throttling my heart, as I watched him inching around to the passenger side, bracing onto the car for support. I was unaware of the extent of his physical decline because he disguised it well in front of me; in front of all of us. I witnessed it, clearly, for the first time. I couldn't deny it any longer.

One particularly trying day for both of us; again, I was driving…to his doctor's appointment, to the bank, to the pharmacy and the grocery store. He loved driving but his ability was impaired due to his recent seizure. One more pleasure he had to relinquish.

I was nervous with him directing me, complaining about my driving and my confusion at getting to places around town. But I dismissed his comments, avoided potholes and tried not to upset him as we approached the doctor's office.

He had no patience with me today.

He refused my help, insisting that he had to put on his own protective gloves and mask. I ignored it and concentrated on setting up the wheelchair to wheel him into the office.

"I'm one of Jerry's kids…he spouted. "Just call me Stephen Hawking."

I sank into his frustration at the loss of his abilities, the loss of his independence, his need to rely on others for everyday tasks.

When we arrived back home, Jon was exhausted and ready to lie down, but my other brother Joe was already present and needed to get some tools out of the shed for a project he was working on, so Jon had to delay his rest and address this.

Jon explained to me in detail where the specific nails were kept on the back porch but I misunderstood his directives and brought out the wrong batch.

He snapped at me in front of Joe, "Not those ones! You didn't listen to me!"

And then more emphatically to Joe, "Jesus, she never listens!"

Ashamed and humiliated I fought back tears. After a long trying day, I collapsed. Joe gave me a sympathetic look as if to say, *"he doesn't mean it. He can't help it."*

I know Jon's struggle with loss of control and independence was insurmountable. And I understood his intolerance…but it still hurt deeply.

…Before he got sick, it was a few days after Bill, my mother's second husband, had died, and Jon and Joe came over to Mom's because she was getting rid of Bill's clothing and wanted them to take what they liked. I was lying on the bed in the spare bedroom exhausted from the week ordeal I had had with my mother at Gosnell Hospice House, so I was feeling a bit punchy. Also, a little edgy and resentful because I had just spent the last week at Bill's bedside, for Mom, for HER husband. I did more for him at the end than I did for my own father which I still have a twinge of guilt about.

Both brothers were trying on all kinds of coats and jackets of Bill's and every one of them fit and looked good on Jon. They looked good on Joe too. Although six years apart in age, my brothers were so similar in physique and looks they could have been twins.

Jon was a clothes horse. He couldn't turn down a thing. There was even an old pair of navy-blue gym shorts with an elastic waistband that he tried on and wanted. He was talking a mile a minute, had me in stitches with his running commentary and back and forth banter with Joe.

He was telling us about the time Lisa went shopping for him at Marlins when they were having a sale. Marlins is a discount store located in the 60's time-warp Downeast Maine town of Skowhegan, (*Skow-Vegas*, as Jon would call it). For a set price it was "take away whatever you can fit in a suitcase." He described the "buys" Lisa would get there, brand name items at dirt cheap prices. And she'd roll each item of clothing up into a tiny tube, that way, packing in as much as possible. She'd bring home a suitcase full of clothes for him. Even HE would have to cross his arms in the air and give Lisa the sign indicating, "stop, time out…enough!"

6

MY BIRTHDAY SURPRISE

It was October 2018. For my birthday, Bruno and I were planning on spending a long weekend in Carmel, New York at the Downey's country home. What a great getaway it was for us. Nancy Downey was a generous client, always offering me the use of her home there when they were away. It was a luxury nine bedroom/nine bath estate with lovely gardens and grounds and a private tennis court that we had the privilege to enjoy, and we liked to take advantage of it whenever possible. We used it many times, with family members, with friends or just by ourselves. It was only 90 minutes outside of the City and we'd be in the country.

"I wonder what the poor people are doing today," my sister Jan would say while lounging around the firepit drinking wine.

Jon spent several weekends with us there with friends and with family. He drove my father to it several times and we got to enjoy playing tennis and softball together while Dad was still healthy. Blessed memories.

Jon and Bruno at the fire pit, Downey's house, Carmel, New York

Joe and Jon playing their ukuleles around the fire pit, Carmel, New York

We befriended the caretaker John and his wife Madeleine, who lived in their own house, right next door on the property. They were good people and we often included them in our gatherings.

This was a perfect opportunity for Jon and Lisa to come and join us for a gorgeous fall weekend. Just us four. We could cook up some nice meals; have a great time bonding over our shared interests such as our love for film and music, discussing the mysteries of the universe together under the stars around the fire pit at night.

It was easy for Bruno and I to connect with Jon and Lisa on a deeper level. Our conversations were rich and fulfilling. We could laugh and talk about the silliest things too, like reminiscing about 60's TV shows and the candy that was popular when we were kids. Sharing all our favorites like Red Hots, Teaberry and Beaman's gum. And remember those candy cigarettes? What the hell did we do with those? Pretend we were smoking them?

We could go for walks down to the reservoir, and at night, watch some movies together on the big screen in the den. I was hoping they could join us. Just us four. What a treat for my birthday.

I texted Jon to see if he could sneak away, without telling the rest of the family, so they wouldn't be hurt for not being included on the invite. Jesus, we're all adults now, but I still feel guilty if I don't invite everyone for fear of hurting someone's feelings. We're such a close knit (enmeshed) family, everyone seems to know everyone's business and whereabouts and God forbid we don't tell Mom what's going on.

Jon texted back that he would be up in Perry, at his beloved coastal camp getaway that weekend and Lisa would be away too, visiting with her mom in Skow-Vegas, so they wouldn't be able to join us. Too bad.

I was drinking a glass of wine, sitting out at the fire pit and he called to wish me a happy birthday. That's what we always did; called each other on our special day and spoke for an hour or two. We hardly talked on the phone the rest of the year, except for this day and on holidays, but it was always as if we had just spoken recently and no time had passed.

That's what I loved about our relationship. We were close even though we didn't stay in touch by phone. We chatted for a while and in the midst of the conversation, he mentioned he was having some real trouble with his wrist. I didn't think too much about it and made light of it, since he had had wrist issues in the past from all the physical labor he did and often, we would discuss our ailments. I had been studying Homeopathy so I suggested he try the remedy Ruta which is specific to wrist joint problems.

Later that week it got worse and I suggested the problem might be originating from a pinched nerve in his neck. He made an appointment with a doctor and they did an x-ray of his neck but found nothing amiss.

The following week when Lisa came back home, she noticed that he was dragging his right leg. She quickly called her friend, an Osteopath, and he examined him. That doctor was the one who said the issue was coming from Jon's head and to go to the emergency ward immediately.

It was on a Wednesday and the culprit; a brain tumor, was discovered through imaging, and Jon needed surgery as soon as possible.

I believe someone above was looking out for him: the top brain surgeon in the area happened to be available and performed surgery on him at Maine Medical Center in Portland the very next day.

Jon went into that surgery, knowing that he might not survive and had made the decision with Lisa not to tell any of us what was going on until after the procedure. I could have killed him for this. But they both must have been in shock and were trying to keep things as normal as possible by not dragging the whole family into their personal hell.

That was always my brother's way. To go it alone. To isolate and not ask for help. Even with his marriage to Lisa. She lived upstate most of the time and he insisted he was fine with this.

I never believed him.

It was late Friday afternoon when I got a phone call from Joe and he said, "sit down, I have some news to tell you." And then he repeated with his voice cracking, "Are you sitting down?"

My heart was in my mouth as I responded, "Yes."

He started crying as he began telling me about Jon.

I'm a delayed feeler and it took me a moment to register and digest his words. At first, I felt my mouth go dry and my insides froze with shock and disbelief. My teeth started chattering uncontrollably but I was sweating at the same time. I felt nauseous and faint.

Lisa had called Joe after Jon's surgery and shared the good and bad news. It was a brain tumor—Glioblastoma, the worst kind of brain cancer, but Jon had made it through the surgery remarkably well. And at this point they both would be limiting contact with most family members in their need for privacy and peace so they could digest this new information, recover from the shock and emotional trauma without having to navigate through everyone else's pain, and to begin to absorb and sort out the next right action steps. Joe was to relay this information to the rest of the family.

We were all in shock and disbelief. What?! Glioblastoma? I had never even heard of it! I was frantic with fear, with worry, with concern for my brother, for the unknown, a million questions were swirling around in my head, shouting at me. *How could this be? How could it have happened? He was the youngest of us all. It's not supposed to happen this way! What caused it? What is it? How can we heal him? Is there a cure? Cancer? Brain cancer?* It was so scary. I was in anguish. *No no no it just can't be true, the words screamed in my head. There's gotta be some mistake.*

We were all heartbroken. I needed answers and information but this is when Google and Web MD are dangerous. I immediately called Lisa to say I was coming up to Maine and wanted to be there with her and Jon and with the family to help out any way I could.

At first, Lisa and Jon insisted they wanted to be left alone with no help from family.

Jon had a large folk-art print of a golf course scene hanging over the fireplace in his living room. My Dad and Jon were very close and shared their love of golf. Lisa revealed the night after Jon's surgery, while she was lying alone upstairs in bed, that painting fell off the wall and landed on the floor in front of the fireplace, glass shattering into pieces. It was as if someone took it off the wall and smashed it down on the floor. She believes it was my Dad, sending her a message loud and clear from beyond the grave. *"Call in the troops for God's sake! Ask the family for help!"*

When I got to Maine, while Jon was still in the hospital, we all joined forces and thoroughly cleaned and cleared out his married bachelor pad to make it comfortable and safe for his return home in a few days, since Lisa had been living upstate and he had been left to his own devices (not being the best at housekeeping, by any means). We cleared things out and moved furniture around to make it wheelchair friendly. Joe had moved Jon's large bed downstairs to the living room area since Jon was incapable of walking, let alone climbing stairs to the second-floor bedroom, and Joe built a makeshift handicap ramp on the back steps so we could wheel him up and into the house. We were all hoping and praying he would get the use of his legs back. They said he might. He worked hard, it took time, and he did.

We were all there cheering him on in the driveway when he came home from the hospital. The air was palpable with tension, overwhelmingly fraught with anxiety and heavy hearts but everyone tried their best to be positive, light, nonchalant, supportive and upbeat. Our hearts were bleeding as we witnessed Jon struggle with his faculties. He couldn't stand on his own two feet and we couldn't get the wheelchair up the ramp. So, Joe, Bruno and our nephew Ryan supported him under each arm and carried him while the rest of us helped with his feet and legs, as best we could, to walk him up and into the house to his bed. We had lit the woodstove and had a nice warm fire going, trying to make things as cozy and comfortable as possible for his homecoming.

And then…although we hated to leave, we left them alone to give them time to get settled in, rest and recover before beginning to explore the next way forward.

It would be the start of a 46-month massive ordeal and undertaking for Jon, and for Lisa, his wife and primary caretaker; to learn, to research, to sift through all the information, discuss the pros and cons, and make hundreds of scary decisions about follow up treatments; for radiation and chemotherapy, for more surgeries that were ultimately needed, and to educate themselves and decide on all the additional resources and options for complementary healing treatments and modalities that were available to them to help him on his healing journey. Making mistakes and then adapting and adjusting to outcomes, finding out what did and didn't work mainly through trial and error, since everybody reacts differently to treatments. Always seeking the best possible decisions in the hopes of gaining the ultimate possibility of healing for Jon.

7
FUNNY STUFF

Jon was the family mascot and comedian, and we could always count on him to shift tension and lighten mood. When he wasn't sick or tired, (which, over the years, was often), he was fun, engaging and entertaining and had a wicked dry sense of humor.

Adored by relatives, always the last to leave any family reunion, he could engage with an elderly aunt and patiently listen to her as if she were the only person in the room.

Jan hosted the DiMauro family reunion one summer at her backyard pool. It was a potluck feast with all our favorite Italian dishes; lasagna, manicotti, meatballs, sausages, salads galore, cannolis, homemade cookies and my aunt Ginny's potent Ba-Ba rum cake…one bite would make your eyes water. (Her husband Lee confessed; he had snuck into the kitchen, taste tested the batter, and decided it needed something more…another generous douse of rum.)

We had set up a microphone and speakers. My Dad and his brothers all played string instruments and loved to perform.

To loosen up the crowd, Ryan started things off with some Bert & I jokes, mimicking that breathy Downeast Maine accent:

lob-stahs over hee-yah…ayah, yah, yah, yah!" and my father was up next…twanging on his guitar and singing country western songs.

Dad was mid-stream through a soulful tune, when all of a sudden, Jan came running out of the house in full Cher regalia… having been a huge fan of hers, she'd acquired several outfits and wigs and been entering (and winning!) Cher look-alike contests around town… grabbed the mike, upstaged my father, and started belting out "If I Could Turn Back Time."

The reaction from the crowd was less than enthusiastic. Everyone ceased chattering. Looked on with blank stares, dumbfounded, not quite knowing what to make of this display.

Without missing a beat, Jon turned to the gang and pleaded in a Jack Benny deadpan… "Folks…PLEASE come back."

Jon jumping off the diving board at Jan's pool party-always the life of the party

One year, we went on a family cruise for Thanksgiving, and Jon, open, curious and genuinely interested in people, easily chatted with the dining room maître d and the ship captain. A renaissance man, he had the ability to find commonality and converse with folks from all walks of life.

Lisa and he traveled the Maine county fair circuit to sell her handmade jewelry. Jon, with his warm infectious personality, was a clever salesman, adept at luring folks into their booth.

"I stand out front," he'd tell me, "And as someone approaches, I make a suggestion of a piece they might like, allow them to try it on, then walk away and leave them alone, while keeping an eye on them so nothing is stolen."

It worked. People appreciated his no pressure sales technique, could sense his authenticity and trusted him. The craft shows were successful and the most lucrative aspect of their business.

Lisa and Jon at their booth at the craft show

I loved that he and I could talk about anything. He was open and authentically honest.

I've kept all our text exchanges over the past four years. We'd share photos of birds, what he had for lunch, pictures of him and Lisa at his camp Downeast, beautiful sunsets, current events and articles of our mutual curiosities and interests like natural wonders and strange archeological sites that can't be explained, the Wimbledon finals, investments, and of course jokes; funny photos and ridiculous articles like one on goat yoga and toilet humor galore. I texted him a photo of a book titled "Can Holding in a Fart Kill You?" His dry response, "You tell me? It is not something you regularly do."

While riding the bus up to Maine from the City I texted him photos of treats I was bringing him.

"Tell the driver to step on it," Jon replied. "I got a bad case of crs (can't remember shit). Also, cfs (can't find shit)."

Or in our discussion of planetary alignments, "Is it retrograde to Uranus?" he'd ask me.

"Actually, Saturn squares Uranus on June 14th," I explained and Jon's reply, "Ouch baby."

And I have kept several videos of him sharing funny stories. I love that I can pull them up on my phone occasionally and see him and hear his voice. He'd crack me up with his back-and-forth dry banter. Like our exchange on the latest insanity from wellness influencers—"Perineum sunning."

I quoted from the article, "they claim in a mere 30 seconds of sunlight on your perineum, you will receive more energy from this than you would in an entire day being outside with your clothes on."

He replied, "Sounds like bullshit to me."

I joked, "Puts an end to the expression, 'you can stick it where the sun don't shine.'"

He confirmed, "Adds new meaning to it for sure."

I kept at it, "I'd be afraid a bee would sting me, or a mosquito would fly in."

His dry response, "only a 30 second window of opportunity." And then more philosophically, "People are searching…go out on the patio— let me know if it works."

And when he had his second craniotomy and he sent me pictures of his "latest beauty mark," a Frankenstein incision on his forehead, I looked upon the crack as another opening to allow the divine to enter in for complete recovery, healing and remission.

"Why not?" he responded, always leaning towards the positive.

And our deeper exchanges.

"Jon, you getting sick has given us all an opportunity to heal. I'm sorry you were the one and that it happened to you and not me (or Mom), but I thank you. You are the messenger. I wouldn't have heard the message if it happened to Mom. I know that's not comforting but I thank you for being the impetus for change."

He replied, "It is okay. I needed to "get sick" to continue on my healing journey. No one knows how long they have…I feel like I can live many years in acceptance and appreciation."

I said, "I do too! You will outlive us all; I believe now that you see and live in the light!"

I wanted to believe this.

Jon said, "I am very grateful for a loving sister like you and of course Lisa. We talk like this. I know I have helped her."

"Yes, I'm sure you have," I said. "She is healing her soul so much on this journey too. Thanks to you."

"I want for very little," he said. "I ask for continued healing and spiritual growth. I am blessed with an abundance of riches. Thank you for all your prayers and light you bring to the planet. It resonates on and on."

Jon, me, Jan, Joe (the sibs)

8

CONNECTIONS

May 3, 2023

We went up to Maine for the weekend to gather with family for the first time since Jon's death. My mother had a Mass at St Peter's in honor of what would have been his 63rd birthday, and then we went to brunch, just us sibs with Bruno and Mom. It's been eight months since he left us and I haven't been to Maine since his memorial in September last year. It doesn't feel the same there without him.

I feel flat around my family without Jon. We were all attracted to his light, gravitating towards him like plants to the sun. He was the glue that held our family together. I tried my best, but I was dissociated and bored with everyone and their conversations, talking about their lives. It was exhausting. Everyone means well, we just don't quite know how to communicate without his lead.

Jon was the lifeline of the party for us all and then he'd need to go away up north to his camp for a week to recover in silence. He'd always been this way—even before he got sick—needing solitude as much as socialization. And he had a habit—sometimes in our presence, of closing his eyes while talking. I noticed him doing it more often as his disease progressed. I think it was his way of shutting out all the distractions of others; going within so he could focus on what he wanted to convey. Or maybe he was just tired. Tired of all our energies. I get that. I find myself doing that now when I need to go within too.

Jon became even more sensitive to noise as his cancer progressed and he found the sound of clinking pans and utensils while I cooked for him, excruciating. It was a challenge to maintain the level of quiet his brain needed. I was extra careful when closing creaky doors and tiptoed around in slippers walking through the house. The static of family interaction was jarring and we were a LOUD family. Lisa was loud too yet creative in coming up with fun and clever ways to help him cope—like with noise muting earmuffs.

Jon's noise-muting earmuffs

My father had a special affinity with his youngest son Jon. Their connection was unique and strong; they'd always been close. They had the same hands and similar expressions. When talking with Lisa on the phone, Jon would lovingly call her "dear," a term of endearment my Dad often used.

Years ago, when my father was sick with end stage bladder cancer and was living in South Portland, Maine, on Broadway, in an apartment by himself, I visited with him that last August of his life. I was cooking dinner for us and making him nasty superfood green drinks; trying desperately to heal him too.

Dad was sitting in the Lazy Boy chair we had bought for him and thought he'd heard Jon walking up the driveway. "Here he is!" he beamed. I looked out the window but it wasn't him, only a passerby.

It reminded me of when we were kids and we'd visit our grandparents. Grandma would be sitting in a chair looking out the window of their 2nd story tenement apartment, anticipating our arrival and Grandpa would be across the street hanging out on the corner with his cronies, the street gang of elders. As soon as he recognized our car approaching, he'd hobble over to the apartment and Grandma would see us, smile and wave from the window too.

Jon and I would occasionally sleep-over. It was a big deal spending the night in Portland…felt strange and unfamiliar but we had each other for camaraderie and comfort.

In place of our suburban backyard, we'd play tag outside on their back porch, challenging each other to peak down over the railing to the city street below, or run up and down the front stairwell, sneaking up to the 3rd floor where "the ghosts" lived… with smelly old people stuff everywhere…we'd dare each other to sniff the cushioned seats of the chairs, and scrounge through the living room table drawers where my grandfather always kept hard candies and packages of Wrigley's and Doublemint gum. In the morning, not wanting to hurt their feelings, we'd choke down the soft runny eggs before Dad came to pick us up. Always leaving wealthier with a quarter and a pack of gum in our pockets; a treat from Grandpa, whenever we came to visit.

I'm happy Jon, you and Dad are together now. I think of you both blissfully living out your days, playing golf, eating, laughing, talking, listening to music...you playing your ukulele and dad on his guitar, with Grandma and Grandpa smiling, looking on too."

When I imagine this is the way it is, it soothes my heart.

Nicki, Dad, Jan, me, Jon in 2009

9

DAD'S HELPERS

When we were young, in addition to his day job, my father was always moonlighting to make ends meet. One of his gigs was setting up and taking down the Saturday night "Beano" game in Redbank, South Portland at the community center. I have no clue why it was called "Beano" instead of Bingo. It was the same game. He made $20 cash. In today's standards, it might be considered slave labor but back in the 60's it was a decent side job.

We would often go with Dad to help him set up on Saturday afternoons. The payoff for us was we could run around on stage, pound on the piano keys, I'd practice performing dance routines, or we'd play tag, racing throughout the building. Dad didn't mind and let us hooligans run wild. But the best part was raiding the concessions for soda and candy.

Dad had a key to the kitchen, and we figured out how to pull out a drawer, gaining access to the precious candy container that was under lock and key. But at some point, they found out about the stolen candy bars and Dad had to pay back money for our misdemeanors.

The soda racks were lined up in the kitchen as well, and Dad would let us each have one after we finished work. Apparently, these weren't under the same scrutiny as the candy. It was a treat because soda was off limits at home, except for on our birthdays when we were allowed to choose our favorite flavor. (I always chose cream soda on my special day.)

For "Beano" we'd have to set up long tables and chairs which were stored on large rolling carts, wheel them out and drag the tables off the cart one at a time. We learned from Dad a technique of opening the ends of the table, locking the legs in place in the open position, and then standing to the side of it, centering ourselves in the middle, and with one swift kick, we'd flip the table upright. We were scrawny teenagers. How the hell did we have the strength to do this? (Attempting this trick recently with a massage table, I threw my back out.)

Then we'd set each table up with six folding chairs, three on each side. And the last thing was flinging a few large tin ashtrays on the tables. That's it. Complete. We could put it together rather quickly.

Tearing down was another story. We'd go there on Sunday mornings. What a mess the place was and it stunk like stale cigarettes. Full ashtrays, trash, Beano chips all over and underneath the tables. If we were lucky, we might find some spare change.

We'd have to stack all the chairs on carts, then empty the ashtrays, clean off the tables, and then tip the tables over on their sides, unfold the legs and stack them on the large rolling carts. Lastly, we'd use the big brooms and sweep the whole place clean. It was quite a job for very little money, but it helped. And we helped Dad, sometimes with pleasure, sometimes grudgingly. And Joe, who had his driver's license by then, once in a while, would do the job on his own when Dad was unable to.

IO

WE'LL ALWAYS HAVE THE BAT

Summer 2021

Rather than sleeping upstairs, the bed I was to use had been set downstairs, perpendicular to Jon's, in the next room so I would be close by if he needed anything. I was taking over for Lisa, giving her a caregiver's break.

We'd chit chat into the night as we were falling off to sleep. I liked that. Sharing last minute thoughts from the day or exchanging some funny stories from our childhood.

Jon had drifted off to sleep, and I wasn't ready, so I opened my iPad and watched something on Netflix with my earbuds in. Lights were all off.

At one point I swore I felt a large bug hit my arm as it flew by, maybe a moth or something attracted to the light of the iPad. I flicked my arm away and forgot about it.

The next night after dinner, as we sat at the kitchen table having one of our marathon nine letter Scrabble games, Jon suddenly jumped up and shut the inside door to the back porch.

"What the hell!" I said, "I haven't seen you move that fast in years!" It's been three years now with his Stage 4 brain cancer.

He had spotted a bat whizzing around and managed to trap it in the back porch vestibule. Adrenaline must have kicked in.

"Oh Jesus," I said. "Now what?" We looked for it through the glass door to see where it had landed but couldn't locate it.

It scudded toward us and banged into the glass door. It scared the hell out of me and I screamed, which scared the shit out of Jon. The little bastard was fast!

We both laughed. "Go in the other room and lie down! Sit Ubu, sit!" he ordered me.

And continued schooling me, "Bats don't want anything to do with you. There's a glass door between us. What'd ya think, it's going to fly right through it?"

In order to set the bat free, he needed to open the outside door of the porch, which was locked from the inside. This meant he had to open the inside door, quickly scoot in and shut the door behind him without the bat fluttering back into the house.

I took a large beach towel and held it up to block the bat in case it tried to fly back in. I prayed it wouldn't. I was so skeeved I'd panic, didn't want to be a wuss, but was ready to drop everything and run.

Once more, Jon bolted into the porch, shut the door behind him and opened the outside door so it could fly away.

"Where'd it go?" he asked. We couldn't find him. Then Jon spotted him prone on the window ledge. He took a stick and shooed it outside the door. It hissed. Sci-fi creepy like!

I doubled over howling with laughter as my brother mimicked the fly, "Lu-ceeeel, Lu-ceeel," imitating an episode from one of our childhood Friday afternoon Creature Features based on the original movie, "The Fly," in which an eccentric scientist's experiment goes wrong. In this version, a fly gets into the teleport machine, and the guy ends up as a fly with a man's head. He then gets trapped in a spider web and keeps calling out to his wife Lucille to save him, in a high-pitched squeaky fly voice.

We finally settled down in the living room to watch a movie. It was some Chuckie doll type of movie where you're waiting for someone to pop out of a closet with a knife. Totally unsettling.

"It's only a movie, just relax."

Sure. Thanks a lot.

Ominous music was playing as she crept into the room. I screamed and jumped six inches off the couch. Ok. Seven.

"That's it," Jon said flatly, and changed the channel to something benign like a rerun of The Walton's.

Later on, Lisa recorded him telling the bat story in great detail to the gang, acting out every part. I saved the video on my phone and every now and then I watch it. One of our last adventures together.

II

MY 50TH CELEBRATION

July 2006

For my 50th birthday we took a sibling, niece and nephew trip to Colorado, since I was gifted the use of my client's home in Keystone. Her place was another sprawling nine bedroom, nine bath mansion set on top of a mountain, with a full-size gym, a wraparound track above it, badminton court, bicycles, an indoor swimming pool, steam room and several whirlpools on various outdoor decks. It was July so the weather was perfect for outdoor exploring, hiking and biking on the mountain and lake side trails. The altitude was well above sea level, so it took some getting used to. We felt short of breath climbing stairs but gradually became accustomed to the change.

Gorgeous mountains with wildflowers in bloom, it was God's country. We took a few day trips with the whole group to explore the area and marvel at the scenery and sights, immersed ourselves in the steaming baths at the Colorado Hot Springs, visited the quaint town of Breckenridge, and rode the chair lift to the peak of a mountain where we all disembarked and stood around in awe, soaking in the greatness of the United States at the

Continental Divide. But Jon and I were the only ones who wanted to do a longer road trip to the Colorado National Monument at the Utah border.

We mapped it out the night before. It was 2006, long before GPS or Google maps. Jon drove the white van that was left for our use, and we got up early and took off for the park.

In the desert in Utah, it was suffocatingly hot, to the point of being dangerous, and it didn't feel safe for hiking. No wonder the park seemed empty. We saw a guy on a bike pedaling up a mountain road and I marveled at how conditioned he must have been to exercise at this altitude and in this heat and wondered how the hell he could do it? We'd stop and step out of the van at various scenic overlooks but that was the extent of our exposure to the extreme heat, and hiking down into the canyon was out of the question.

The whole experience was otherworldly; red rock mountains as far as the eye could see. The stillness and the quiet. Not a soul in sight. It was mystical, awe inspiring; we felt like the only two people on earth. Speechless with the wonder that struck us; indescribable mixed emotions bubbling up. My heart swelled with this aching beauty, with exaltation, with sadness.

I had the same experience witnessing two lions mating in the Serengeti. Tom, Marlene, Tara, (my safari traveling companions) and I, grew silent as our eyes welled up with tears and we rode in silence, privately contemplating this shared sacred encounter.

...Another memorable trip was two weeks sailing in the Virgin Islands with Jon, Joe and his wife Ursula. I went in place of Jon's girlfriend Vicki, who was unable to go at the last minute. Lucky me.

It was my first time sailing in the Caribbean and although Jon and Joe had taken lessons, they were still novice sailors. Ursula and I were completely ignorant but willing to follow orders and go along for the adventure. I remember we let the sails out full, were cruising along at a good clip, the weather was beautiful and the sun was shining.

Then one of us casually pointed ahead and said, "what's that cloud covering?" And before you knew it, we were caught up in a massive rain and windstorm and the boat almost capsized. We immediately dropped all sails, and the boat made a 360-degree turn around and right sided itself. Although quite shook up, we recovered. Hell, we were on vacation. Nothing bad could happen to us here in paradise.

We had chartered our own boat from St. Thomas and Jon and I shared a bunk together at the bow. I never quite got my sea legs and was slightly seasick the whole trip, but I didn't let that prevent me or us from having one of our best adventures together. My stomach was a bit queasy, and I'm sorry to say my digestive system let it be known by the foul-smelling gas I was releasing on a regular basis, especially at night. *Sorry Jon.*

But when I go on a trip, the bad stuff dissipates in my memory, and I only retain the good. What an amazing trip. We felt like Robinson Crusoe and sailed around to all the different U.S. and British Virgin Islands. It was May 1992 and not as crowded back then at this time of year, especially at the smaller islands like Salt, Peter and Jost Van Dyke.

Sometimes we'd be the only ones moored in a harbor. At Salt Island, Joe and Ursula took the dinghy to the shore to go for a walk and Jon and I stayed on the boat and did what we loved best —sunning, swimming and snorkeling.

The Caribbean Sea is crystal clear aquamarine, and the underwater life is exquisite. The salt content makes for extreme buoyancy, and you can float forever. We were both enraptured—a throwback to when we were kids and we'd play "Sea Hunt" in my brothers' bedroom.

...We loved watching that show of underwater adventures starring Lloyd Bridges. Mimicking the show by making up some scenario and pretending the bunk bed was the boat, we'd "dive" off the bed to the floor and simulate swimming around underwater, by crawling on the floor, holding our breath the whole time we were off the "boat." We'd copy the actors' behavior and dialog from the show. Before Jon took off for a "dive," I'd grab his arm and say with concern, "Be careful."

Or we'd climb from the "boat" (the bed) to the other furniture (the desk and chairs), seeing how far we could get around the room and stay "above water."

As youngsters at Pine Point Beach in Scarborough, Maine, we'd wade into the freezing ocean, throw a piece of driftwood further out into the waves and yell "my baby!" forcing us to emerge deeper in, to save "the baby" and acclimate our bodies to the frigid water. Eventually we'd get the courage to submerge ourselves completely.

Now in the warm waters of the Caribbean Sea, we recreated our "Sea Hunt" and "The Under Sea World of Jacque Cousteau" fantasies, for real.

Jon had Reggae music playing and we enjoyed the luxury of lounging on the boat, by ourselves, in this tropical paradise and then when we needed to cool off, we'd put on our snorkeling gear, climb down the ladder, and push off the boat. Floating all the way to the coral reefs, we'd swim through beautiful multi-colored schools of fish and explore plant life. If he spotted something interesting, he'd turn and face me directly under water, with eyes as big as saucers, excitedly point out and indicate his find to me. We were like giddy little children.

We sailed to the various islands, ate conch on Jost Van Dyke and explored and hiked around St. John's, waded through the Baths on Virgin Gorda, where a local climbed a tree barefoot and picked us fresh mangoes to eat. We peeled them with our hands and gorged ourselves in the sticky sweetness of these island delights, right there on the beach. Ahhh…native. Glad we had dental floss back on the boat.

The surf and the beaches were magical—pristine and deserted, just how we liked them—our Gilligan's Island.

We found outdoor showers at one spot and luxuriated in hot soapy shampoos, exquisitely indulgent after our minimal cold rinse offs on the boat: necessary to conserve our water supply. Simple pleasures. Ursula took a picture of us; and Jon, always the jokester, suggested we flash moons.

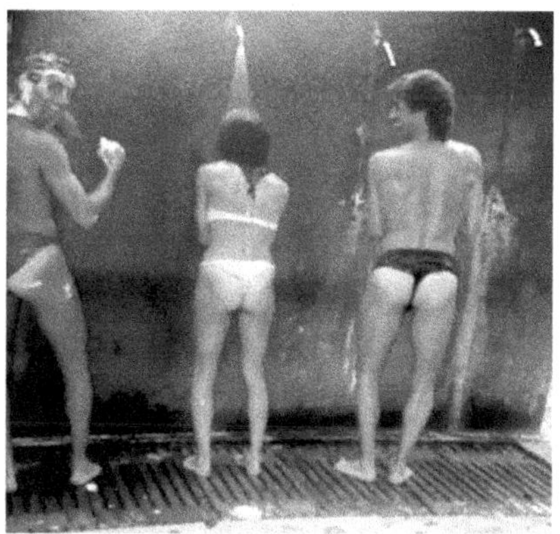

A trip etched in my memory forever.

I 2

FOOD & SUMMER OUTINGS WITH JON

August 2021

August in Maine can get hot and humid. When I was caregiving Jon, we planned to attempt an excursion to the shore. I'd prepared everything that morning; packed up a lunch of tuna, veggies, some healthy snacks, water, ice coffee, loaded up the car and we headed to Ferry Beach in Scarborough. I had checked it out earlier on my own and saw that it might be possible to get Jon down to the shore without too much trouble.

The attendant at the gate was an old friend of Jon's. He winked and waved us in, free of charge, saying, "your brother Joe paid for you earlier." We parked in the handicap spot which was close to the entrance to the beach and only a short walk on the soft sand where I could set up chairs at the shoreline.

Teetering a bit on wobbly legs, Jon was able to manage without too much difficulty. Although statuesque at six feet tall, he was weak, so I helped him as best I could, and then set up chairs while he stripped off his Optune head device, taking a much-needed break from the uncomfortable metal head arrays contraption he wore constantly, (which was to prevent brain cancer from growing). This way he could enjoy being out in the hot sun without the apparatus' beeper going off, which sounded like a truck backing up, whenever it overheated. One less thing to deal with.

It was a perfect beach day and the only place to be for some relief from the heat, so I suggested we move the chairs into the water, sit in the ocean and cool off. The cove here was calm. An easy place to put in.

I kept a wary eye on the tide and as it was coming in, I grew concerned about how to get him up and out of the chair and back to dry land, due to his unsteady legs.

Jon, always social and friendly with strangers, chatted with a man and his wife, (who were vacationing from Serbia), about the U.S. open and their hometown tennis star, Novac Djokovitch.

I was distracted. This man must have read my thoughts. He leaned over and whispered, "If you need help, just let me know."

The beach had gotten crowded by now and when it came time to get Jon out of the water, he was struggling to stand, his feet sinking in the soft soaked sand. I told him to lean forward, nose over toes, and "don't look down" into the water since it would throw his balance off.

Humiliated with his loss of physicality and athleticism, he leaned forward in the chair, as I helped steady him with one arm and guided him up by the back of his shorts with my other hand, giving him a wedgie in the process.

He was up! We slowly and deliberately waded through quicksand water to the shore with all eyes glued on us watching our every move. I wanted to scream out, *"PEOPLE…PLEASE… talk amongst yourselves and focus elsewhere!"*

I moved the chairs back to dry land and feeling spent and shaky, we sat down, nerves frazzled. We took a few moments to recover, then ate lunch.

When it was time to go, weak and tired from the sun and the activity, we carefully walked back to the car. I held a towel in front of him as he sat in the driver's seat, stripped off his wet trunks and wrapped a dry towel around himself. I put all the wet, sand-soaked chairs, towels, clothing and coolers in the back of the car.

Jon was driving. After his public display, driving helped restore some sense of dignity and independence.

It was quite an ordeal for me and for Jon, but we loved the fact that we did it—that we pushed past our comfort zones, discovered and achieved a new adventure!

"Let's go again tomorrow!" he exclaimed. I wanted to please him but, honestly, I didn't have it in me. I don't think he really did either. We spent the following day at home, in front of the fans, resting and recuperating.

But…we set wheels in motion. We figured out what was possible. What he was capable of with his disabilities. We wanted to create summer outings for Jon—things that he could do that were fun and would make him feel "normal." Lisa bought a large inner tube so he could now stand in the water with support, while resting his handicap arm afloat. And we found other places with easy access to the shore.

Having scoped out a beautiful breezy point at Two Lights State Park I assumed Jon could walk to, Jan met us there another hot August day and brought lobster meat and smoked oysters which were within his Ketogenic diet. We picnicked at the same place again with Lisa when she came home. "Another great day to be alive!" Jon said.

Jan rented a camp at a lake, a short drive from his house, with easy access to the waterfront. Bruno and I slept over and Jon and Lisa drove up for the day. We all sat on the dock, cooled off in the water sitting in chairs, on floaties, while reminiscing and laughing about old times, cooked up steaks on the grill, and salads and things he could eat. I wanted them to spend the night with us, but it would have been too difficult for Jon.

On holidays and special occasions, Jan would cook him her famous baked hams and roasted turkeys which he loved and were also included in his Keto diet. He'd always say, "I look forward to another Janni ham on the horizon."

Pictures, to me, are life rafts in an ocean of thoughts. I relish the images that highlight these significant memories.

*Jon & sister Jan with her
roasted turkey*

Jan's camp on the lake, August 2021

Two Lights State Park & Ferry Beach, August 2021

13

DOUBLE WHAMMY

Jon was blessed with two years of clear MRIs and then, as was predicted with this disease, another brain tumor developed. At the same time, he was diagnosed with throat cancer. So much all at once.

Apparently, this often is the case. Secondary cancers are common and tend to show up in a person who's immunocompromised.

Each cancer is its own unique disease, so Jon's brain oncologist could not treat his throat. Again, the cancer gods were monitoring. The leading throat cancer specialist in the country, operates using the latest technique in robotic surgery, just so happens to be in Portland, Maine at Maine Medical Center. Jon was in!

His doctors conferred and decided to treat his throat cancer first. He went in for major surgery on December 15, 2020, and would be in the hospital for two weeks. Still in the throes of the COVID 19 pandemic, no one was allowed to accompany patients into the hospital.

Lisa wept as she sat in the car, watching him walk away by himself into the hospital, with his Optune battery pack slung heavily over his shoulder, throwing off his already diminished and fragile gate. Would this be it? Jon marching alone to his death with no one beside him at the end? We were all sick. Terrified. Helpless to do anything.

The surgery and recovery process were horrific. He had to learn to swallow all over again and they were not sure he would regain the use of the necessary throat musculature. It was a slow process, but he did.

After a short round of chemotherapy and as soon as he was strong enough, he went in for his second craniotomy, to remove a rapidly growing tumor in the frontal lobe of his brain. The first tumor had been on the motor strip, causing him to lose physical mobility and the use of his right arm—similar to the effects of a stroke.

The one "blessing" of this tumor was its location. It was in an area of the brain that was considered "low real estate," and would not cause any outward physical damage other than affecting the region of the brain that limits perseveration—"the inability to transition or switch ideas appropriately by repeating words or gestures after they have ceased to be socially relevant." This could be hard to decipher with Jon. He was a natural perseverator. Steadfast. Insistent and stubborn in his opinions and beliefs.

I consider myself a recovered Catholic but all throughout Jon's illness I fervently prayed to Padre Pio, an Italian friar, mystic and venerated patron saint for healing and good health. A Stigmatist, Padre Pio bore the wounds of Christ, which cannot be explained even today. There are numerous stories of miraculous cures through his intercession. Some were healed instantaneously, some gradually, and some experienced not only a physical healing but an inward, emotional and spiritual healing. I hoped Padre Pio would have God's ear and put in a good word for Jon. I wanted to believe in his power; that this was possible.

Brain surgery was scheduled for April 15, 2021, followed by another month of daily radiation treatment. Jon's sheer tenacity, spiritual beliefs and strong will to live carried him through these massive ordeals, leaving him with Frankenstein scars on head and throat, badges of courage.

"It's a great day to be alive," he'd repeat upon awakening every morning.

Jon's stigmatas

I4

A GOOD OMEN

Morning of June 23, 2022

Good morning, Gianni.

I had a great dream about you right before I woke up. You were with Karen, my best friend from the old neighborhood, and Jan and I were meeting you all at the beach. I was running late so I suggested you kill some time and get the car washed, thinking you were riding in Karen's car. We met you at a parking lot at the beach and you both pulled up in separate vehicles. You were in your (or Joe's) old red truck and Karen was in her car — you both had gone through the car wash. You got out of the car and had white jeans on, no shoes and no shirt and all tanned and completely healthy and buffed with the full use of your arm too. I hugged both Karen and you and everyone was acting nonchalant like it was no big deal. I pulled out camera equipment for us to take some photos at the beach and we headed down to the shore. Then I woke up. Maybe this is a good sign.

15

WAITING FOR THE WORD

My favorite niece, Nicki, was in town staying with us for a few days before heading back to California. It was June 29th, 2022, and Jon was going in for his regularly scheduled brain MRI today. We would be notified about the results with a phone call from Lisa, later that afternoon. We were all "in the parentheses," at the precipice of our emotions, teetering on the edge.

He had been on Avastin, the immunotherapy drug of last resort, for the past three months. It seemed to be keeping things at bay. But things were changing.

I could tell when I was with him in Maine a few weeks earlier. He seemed more tired, more withdrawn. I noticed he was perseverating more than usual. We were discussing some news article, and he was repeating his point over and over and could not understand the alternative point I was trying to make.

He was so intelligent! Why couldn't he grasp my simple point…then I caught myself and swallowed the lump in my throat. I realized the cause of his confusion. His brain cancer was growing.

Nicki and I wanted to get outside and bike ride down the Hudson for one last outing before she had to fly back to California that night. We pedaled down to Battery Park and then back up the Hudson and stopped at the Frying Pan for a late lunch. It was a gorgeous clear day to be out on the water.

We had just ordered veggie burgers, fries and beer. As we sat there eating, my cell phone rang. I looked. Lisa. I felt sick to my stomach and my mouth went dry.

Jon's cancer had come back with a vengeance. His oncologist, who had become so fond of them both, cried as she told them there was nothing more that could be done, and prepared them for what to expect in the next five to six weeks. He fought so well for his life and now he was losing it.

Lisa and Jon were devastated. I was to relay the information to the rest of the family as they requested no contact from others right now, so they could retreat and have this precious time to themselves to enjoy the remainder of Jon's life. They planned to spend time at his beloved camp in northern Maine; one last time while he was still able to. Lisa would keep us abreast of Jon's regression and would notify us when it was time to come see him.

I sat there with Nicki. Dumbfounded. Repeating the heartbreaking news. Did I hear Lisa correctly? Was there any possible misinterpretation? I wanted the news from the doctor directly. My mind needed her validity. I couldn't accept the reality of Lisa's revelation.

Reflecting on the truth of Lisa's words, I gradually allowed them to sink in, still scouring every nuance for any possibility of hope. Which wasn't there.

I turned to Nicki, "I have to call your Mom and everyone. They are waiting to hear about Jon."

Nicki is wise beyond her years and hugged me as we both sat there crying.

She said, "Just wait, give yourself some time first, to absorb this information. Make room for YOUR feelings, before sharing with everyone else and taking on the burden of all their emotions."

Basically, put your oxygen mask on first. Sound advice.

We shared our feelings, distraught over the news, and picked at our lunch before getting back on our bikes and heading home.

What follows is a blur. I don't remember when or who I spoke to after that. I was hollow. Lost. Devastated.

I wanted to be with Jon, with both of them, to help in any way. As if I could do anything to save him. The helplessness was unbearable.

Although I have conflicted feelings about Jon's wife Lisa, I respect the diligent and unrelenting care and support she provided for him during the 46 months of his illness. She went from being absent, to fully and completely present. I realize that is her personality. She operated best in extremes.

I had always looked forward to her updates about Jon and their life together. My heart would jolt seeing her text, *"Can we talk now?"* feeling anxious yet relieved, to be out of the dark and offered a glimpse into their private world. I'd immediately prioritize and make time and space for her phone calls and long heartfelt conversations. We'd talk regularly throughout this time and became close and connected.

I'd read stacks of books on various topics related to his condition; from cutting edge nutrition books, biographies by people who have healed their cancers, spiritual health books and holistic, complementary and metaphysical approaches to healing, and I joined several support groups on social media for Glioblastoma patients and family members, so I could stay abreast of the latest information on his type of brain cancer. It was the least I could do from afar, since Jon and Lisa had no spare time or energy for it.

I'd compare notes and engage with others going through this illness in real time. And then share what I learned with Lisa, and we would discuss and brainstorm ideas. She would often run this new information by Jon's healthcare team and sometimes they'd make adjustments to his medications or his supplementation, and some of his negative side effects might dissipate. I felt useful. Helpful. The busyness kept my thinking right sided.

Lisa was effervescent and always looking ahead to the next right possible action step on how she could address Jon's condition, his state of mind, his energy and spirit levels for the best help and healing that was out there and available for him. She would earnestly pursue and seek advice and information from her range of healers and healthcare personnel and ceaselessly advocate for his health. Exhaust all possible sources, interview and talk with people in the field to discuss Jon's condition to provide for him the best quality of life. Always striving to seek more answers and potential new remedies and innovative practices that could possibly help him. Never giving up hope.

I KNOW she was depleted. It was more than a full-time job. She relegated her life and artwork to devote herself exclusively to Jon's caregiving needs. I'd take over for five to seven days, every so often, to give her a break and found it all-consuming, completely draining, both physically and emotionally.

Their house was full of charts and notebooks neatly organized, scrupulously highlighted and marked with meticulously kept records of all of Jon's treatments, experiences, and medical sessions. Using her artistic abilities, motivational cards, colorful drawings and inspirational Post-its were displayed all around the house for continuous reminders to help keep his spirits soaring. They were both highly sensitive individuals, astutely aware of outside energies and susceptible to negative effects of news and the media, so they avoided any triggering stressors, and only highly vibrational people were welcomed into their sphere, for Jon's health and for Lisa's sake as well. It was their way of maintaining control and emotional sobriety.

16

REIKI

In my desperate need to help Jon, I learned the art of Reiki, which is a form of energy healing through touch, one can provide, in person, and transmit healing from afar. I trained privately with Maddalena Blanton, a Reiki Master, traveling to her home in New Jersey for months, once/week all during the winter of 2019, and received my certifications in both levels I and II. I'd practice chair Reiki on Bruno at home and like a poster child client, he'd immediately fall asleep.

When I'd spend time with Jon in Maine, sometimes, I'd give him Reiki at the end of the day. He welcomed it—found it healing and comforting and the energy work relaxed me as well. I'd put on some Native American flute music or nature sounds and he would lie on the bed as I administered the hand positions down his body from head to toes, channeling Reiki to him for the highest possible healing for whatever was needed most for him at the time. He was a master receiver and said he could feel the energy in the form of heat coming off my hands entering into his body and usually fell asleep during a session. I felt useful.

The next day he'd be completely spent. Drained. With energy work, like most things, less is more, but, being a novice, I tended to overdo it.

In an abiding area of my mind, I still believed I could heal Jon.

17

THINGS HAVE CHANGED

August 8, 2022

Monday morning the phone rang. I checked. Lisa. "Things are changing. Jon lost control of his leg today. Would we consider coming up to Maine sooner?" she asked.

Of course we would. We had planned on coming the following weekend but quickly made other arrangements, booked an Airbnb and drove up Wednesday. I didn't tell my mother. Otherwise—fifty questions.

Our rental was on a beautiful street down by the ocean but the place was a Hobbit house. The bedroom was up a ladder, in an attic crawl space and you could only sit up in the middle of the bed, otherwise you'd bang your head on the eaves of the roof. We were paying for the location. Didn't matter. We were there to spend as much time as we could with Jon at his house. As much as he and Lisa would allow us to.

We spent hours with him and Lisa on that Thursday, Friday, and Saturday. He was lying down most of the time, quiet, not communicating much. When he did his voice would cut in and out in a hoarse whisper and I could sense how difficult it was for him to speak. Lisa was doing most of the talking. Maybe she was uncomfortable with the silence, trying to stay upbeat and light, for Jon, for her own sake as well as for ours. He still had a voracious appetite and I had brought him all kinds of goodies from Sullivan's Street Bakery and Little Pie Company in New York City.

His face was distorted and swollen and dark circles ringed his eyes but he smiled for Lisa as she snapped a picture of him eating a piece of sour cream apple walnut pie.

At one point he needed to use the bathroom and struggled to get up out of bed. He insisted on no help from us, and Bruno, Lisa and I stood by feeling utterly helpless, just watching him, ready in case he lost his balance and fell.

The last day I saw Jon was Saturday August 13, 2022. Lisa, speaking for Jon now, conveyed to us quietly, there would be no more visitors after today and that Jon wished to die peacefully alone at home with her. I was disturbed by this, trying to digest and accept his wishes, hoping he might change his mind during the course of my stay in Maine.

I spent over an hour giving him Reiki while Lisa sat at the kitchen table drafting a letter for me to share with the family of Jon's last wishes of how he wanted to die. Bruno had been working on a poem in the other room for the past few days and was inspired to share it with Jon and Lisa.

where you sing your love

(for Gianni and Lisa)

silently
a gentle Maine afternoon
frames your window,
you lie napping
in your bed
as your sister blesses with Reiki
the life ebbing in your heart
so tenderly with love,
i hear finches and chickadees
pecking at the shaded feeder
hanging from your lilac bush
outside the kitchen –
you cannot see them, now
but i hear them for you
there
offer them to you
to share this grace, this peace
this unrelenting journey
you are wafting on,
slowly, graciously
to a place lovely
with sunflowers and sage
and saffron sunsets
far beyond Casco tides,
to Perry
where your limbs, eager and joyous
gather in the cool morning hours
close to the foam and spray and clams
of Cobscook Bay,
your footprints irrevocable on the shore where you sing your love
in Lisa's hair, red with fire –
all you ever care to touch
and linger in
kindling on and on in your embrace...

…I wanted time alone with Jon and suggested Lisa and Bruno go out for a drive. Maybe she would like a break? But she didn't take the hint or didn't want to leave his side. *For Christ sakes, my insides were screaming. I've known him a lot longer than you have? 62 years as compared to your 21!* But on the other hand, I understood. These last moments were precious time together. So, while others were within earshot, I told Jon what he meant to me.

"You know you're an inspiration to me. You've always been authentic and real with everyone and never afraid or intimidated to speak your truth, no matter what. I sometimes cowardly followed the crowd just to fit in but you never did that. You have so much courage and integrity, always have had it, and I admire that about you Jon."

I didn't want to tell him he was the one in the family with whom I connected intimately with on a soul level, and that I loved him and would miss him terribly; that life wouldn't be the same here without him for fear I'd break down. So instead, I reminded him of the time we drove to the Colorado National Monument, the two of us. We were on a family vacation staying in Keystone but no one else wanted to do the day trip.

"It was a spiritual experience. I couldn't explain it to them when we got back. They wouldn't understand. But I know you did. I'm glad we shared that together, Jon."

It was difficult for him to talk now. His voice was breaking up but as I reminisced about our day in the desert, he hoarsely whispered something to me I couldn't make out. Lisa could, and translated.

"This magic moment," he said, quoting the line from a song that so perfectly encapsulated the essence of our experience together. *You mirror my soul, Gianni… Namaste.*

Jon at our Colorado National Monument Road trip, July 2006
"This Magic Moment"

18

THE WAITING FOR THE END

As I gave Jon an extended final Reiki treatment in the living/bedroom area, Lisa sat next to Bruno in the kitchen, whispering, so as not to disturb Jon. She drafted a letter to be shared with my family about Jon's end of life wishes.

At one point, Bruno noticed she left the room and came back wearing bright red lipstick. *That's odd*, he thought.

Maybe her lips were dry from all the talking? Or did she feel the need to make herself look more attractive? Or maybe, it's just something she does out of habit.

…When I was a kid, my Mom had a habit of running errands in the car, wearing only her bra and girdle, with a trench coat as a cover-up. In the driveway, she'd adjust the rear-view mirror and I'd watch her apply bright red lipstick and blot it with a tissue. Me, pencil lipped, admired her full Sophia Loren ones. She'd don her dark prescription sunglasses, fluff her hair, readjust the mirror and off we'd go. As co-pilot, I sat in shame and fear she'd be caught half naked or we'd run into someone we knew and they'd guess her secret. I was ready to hop out once we arrived at our destination to quickly complete the task so we could get back home in a hurry without being found out.

Lisa has those same full lips.

It was difficult to hear Jon felt "complete" with family and wanted no further contact with us, once he began to decline, which was happening now. He wished to have his spirit transition with peace and grace at home with only Lisa and his hired aide, Errol, by his side. It was more comfortable for Jon to order Errol around, than to ask and accept help from us. He didn't know him personally. Removing the intimacy must have made it easier for Jon.

Lisa did her best to honor Jon's wishes, keeping the place as quiet as possible, meeting his demands and tiptoeing around in stocking feet. He was extremely sensitive to the slightest variance in noise.

"Less Eh..rol…less Eh..rol," he managed to croak out to her. Apparently, Errol was a talker.

"There is no earthly need to send notices about his ongoing condition. None of that will be communicated," Lisa stated in the letter. We were simply to be notified through an email from her of his passing…Unfathomable…Grueling and difficult directives to swallow.

Lisa texted Bruno later and reiterated what was said in the letter. She wrote:

"Please assist us in maintaining the private vessel that is needed for Jon to now relax in a most deep way, free of interactions outside his chosen inner team of carers.

Today is our last day without others being present, so it is a sacred space. Please make sure Joanne communicates to Jan the details of what we discussed about "no texting" as it jerks Jon's head or mine into memory or need to respond to another…this happens to be a time of TRUE boundary. Simplicity for HIM. If someone has the urge to reach out towards him or to me, please have them burn sage instead.

I do not have the capacity to continue juggling other's hopes. All about Jon's wish for privacy now. He loved the visit today but exhaled when he was alone again in the house. "I need it simple and alone with you now, Lisa."

I reach out due to a text from Jan moments ago trying to continue connecting (which isn't wrong, but that window has been closed out of respect to Jon.)

This is what we absolutely need Joanne to manage for Jon, that our privacy be 100% upheld.

Jon LOVES everyone. Everyone knows this is true.

Essentially, when left in the quiet peace that Jon desires, his spirit builds momentum moving towards his new chapter. This is the GIFT we are giving him, by respecting his wishes. He wants extended peace at home. He feels everyone's love. His view has now shifted to a world beyond ours. We must all give him the freedom to move towards the light path towards his future destination."

19

TELLING MOM

The end of August is the best time to be in Maine, away from the sweltering heat of New York City. Perfect blue skies and ocean waters warm enough to dip into without freezing.

After our Hobbit House stay, Bruno and I moved to my sister's condo for the week. She was away at a lake camp, so we had the place to ourselves and attempted to enjoy our "vacation" doing the usual summer things we love to do in Maine; play tennis, go to the beach, ride bikes, eat seafood and ice cream at our favorite haunts, but my brother's impending death weighed heavily on us. I kept thinking, *I'm here Jon and Lisa. Available for whatever you need.* Hoping they would change their minds and call me. Ask me to come be with them while Jon was dying. Help him cross over. I checked my texts constantly. Silence. No word from them.

After I shared Lisa's letter with Joe, Ursula and Jan, Joe asked me if I could go to Mom and give her the news of Jon's last wishes. *Oh brother...* but it's the least I could do. Joe has borne the brunt of my mother's emotional pain far too long.

Bruno and I drove over to her place on Friday and sat her down at the kitchen table.

"Jon's dying, Mom. And he wants to die in peace at home alone with Lisa and his aides to help him. He feels complete with family and doesn't want to see any of us again." I calmly managed to convey to her.

"What does this mean?" she cried, eyes bulging in disbelief and pain. "I don't understand it. What is he saying? What is Lisa saying? I want to see my son. My son! I want to hold his hand and tell him I love him. I can't bear this. My heart is breaking! It's not possible. I can't accept it."

I too felt the same way but forced myself to advocate for them. "These are his wishes Mom," I pleaded with her. "We have to honor them." And then trying a different approach, "How would you feel if your last wishes were not respected?"

She would have a momentary glimmer of understanding and acceptance, but it would dissipate as quickly as it registered, and she was lost and confused in her anguished grief again. It took every ounce of my emotional strength to not fall apart completely.

We went over it again, she asking me the same questions and me, repeating Jon and Lisa's wishes in as many variations and interpretations I could muster to help her understand.

I *didn't understand. How could I convince her?*

"Let's go to Dock's for dinner." I suggested as a distraction, (a sort of Halley's Comet tactical diversion). "They have great seafood dinners and we can sit outside."

It was a good move. I needed it too. Eating out gave us something else to focus on and we were able to swallow some much-needed sustenance, hopefully helping us to digest this news as well.

"He's very peaceful now and he's not in pain, Mom," I guessed. I lied. Anything to try and put her mind at ease as well as my own.

We stayed with her for the next four days and nights. Joe organized a family gathering at his place on Sunday to celebrate Mom's birthday early since we were planning on driving back to New York City mid-week unless…I heard from Jon and Lisa…

Nothing. So, we reluctantly left Maine, and I cried a good deal of the ride home. Feeling utterly helpless, the waiting, again, was unbearable. This time, I was suffocating *between the parentheses.*

In the meantime, my mother, up to her old manipulative tricks, had crafted a letter to Jon and Lisa, in disguised handwriting, written by one of her aides, and had it dropped off in their mailbox. She figured if they thought the letter was from me, they would open it. Sneaky, disrespectful, yet creative, (I must give her that), her inability to accept Jon's end of life wishes, her relentless pursuit to see him and have her questions answered, were astounding.

I hadn't realized what had occurred until months later when I spoke to Lisa and she asked me about the letter.

"What letter?" I asked, thinking she was referring to the one she and Bruno drafted together, (Jon's last wishes), for me to share with family members.

"No. The letter that you left in our mailbox."

"I never wrote you a letter or sent you anything after you requested us not to."

The revelation was sickening. My only concern was I was afraid Jon died thinking I violated his final wishes.

Lisa tried to console me. "Jon had begun a new medication including morphine the day before the letter arrived. I truly believe the morphine 100% dulled any feelings he might have had contrary to his immense love for you. He adored you. He said, "poor Joanne. It's as though Gloria is channeling right through her…good thing she and Bruno are leaving town."

My tormented mother continued to badger Lisa for answers after Jon's death, even hiring a lawyer to request certain items she had given him be returned, all an attempt to satisfy her insatiable need to know, to settle her mind, or maybe, to find peace? Was it her unconscious need for reconciliation with her son?

20

ALL SOULS' DAY

November 2, 2023

It's All Souls' Day. At this time, some cultures believe the veil between the living and the dead is the thinnest and if ever there is a time to try and communicate with deceased loved ones, this would be it.

"Jan texted me that she dreamt about you, that you were at college, healthy, happy and strong. And then she woke up and found a red cardinal outside her window looking in at her. I reassured her that was you, Jon. Checking in on her. Sending her a message. She's struggling with some issues, and I told her to ask you for help. I believe you ARE in "college," on a higher plane of existence. And if we stay open, we can learn and receive grace from you.

Mom called me and said she was feeling heavy and lost in her grief and I too have been thinking a lot of you lately and feeling down. I'm early for a session with a client so I pop into St Ignatius Cathedral, light a candle for you, say a prayer and listen.

I took a bike ride down the Hudson River Park on one of the last warm days of the year and noticed they are putting in Pickleball courts at 34th Street on the Hudson. Oh c'mon! You know I'm a tennis advocate and not fond of this stepchild to my favorite sport. Couldn't they have put tennis courts out there instead?

I dreamt about you later that night—I was heading downtown to play pickleball. I told you to meet us down at the court and you said you would. You were alive and healthy. I woke up feeling peaceful and unburdened."

November 7, 2023

My 93-year-old client confided in me that she has been dreaming about her deceased mom and feeling sad she's gone. I believe as we get closer to our end here on earth, our relatives or spirit guides come to us for comfort; to help us in our winding down days and to let us know there's something beyond this. I shared that with her, in so many words or less, not to scare her, but to try and console her. I hoped I was able to ease her distraught state. I'm not sure I succeeded. She died a few weeks later.

2 I

THE FIRSTS ARE THE WORST:
FALL APART OR FALL TOGETHER

November 12, 2023

My brother Joe turned 70 this year. I asked his wife Ursula what he would like for his special birthday. She said he'd like for Bruno and me to come up to Maine and celebrate it with him. So, we did. I regret missed opportunities with Jon and Lisa. I don't want more regrets.

We took the bus up and spent the first night at Mom's and then moved over to Joe's in the country and spent the next two nights with him and Ursula. Jan joined us too. It was easy connecting with my siblings.

This will be the second winter since Jon's been gone, second holiday season. The "firsts" are the worst, but the "seconds" are only slightly better. The first two years are considered early-stage grief. As I was walking around TJMAX the other day, Christmas music was playing and all the decorations and gifts were out on display. I started thinking about Jon, about Christmas and how he loved all those special foods and festivities. Holiday memories came flooding back and I started crying right there in the store. That's the thing about grief—you never know when it will sneak up on you.

I was down at the gym exercising and I spotted a trainer giving a radial/ulnar exercise to a client to strengthen her wrist and forearms and just like that, tears started welling up in my eyes. I was back exercising with Jon over FaceTime using that red dowel I sent him to build strength. His muscles would be quivering and shaking but sometimes he'd be able to hold his grip on it and perform a full rotation. Those were on his good days.

…One year when we were kids we got a tape recorder for Christmas. Mom and Dad had hidden it and secretly taped our Christmas morning with all the hubbub and excitement around the opening of the presents. Then they revealed the gift to us and we got to listen to ourselves as they played it back. Wow. What a big deal that was. What a thrill to hear ourselves and how funny we sounded. That recorder was our favorite gift that year and we'd spend hours taping ourselves singing Christmas carols.

The anticipation of Christmas—counting down the days until December 25th, was more fun than the actual day. You and I would spend a lot of time sitting under the tree, next to the presents that were already wrapped and placed there. These were the little gifts we kids bought for each other. I saved money from my allowance all year long to buy mine.

We'd shake them and try to guess what they were and decide which one we would open on Christmas Eve. We could each open up just one. It was a tradition. The other gifts from Santa would arrive on Christmas morning.

While sitting around the tree, we'd sing in rounds "when the green leaves grew all around around around, and the green leaves grew all around!" Remember? It was our version of the song, "And the Grass Grew Green" We'd get to the chorus of the last few verses and we'd do a guttural version of "AAAND the green leaves grew…." Sometimes I sing it now, when I'm alone walking through Central Park.

Once we sat at the kitchen table and taped ourselves singing "The Twelve Days of Christmas" in rounds. You were so young. Maybe five or six. Of course, I tried to direct the whole thing and would point to you or Joe or Jan when it came to each person's verse. Every time I'd point to you to sing the next verse, no matter where we were in the song, you'd always sing "Fiii—ve Golden .... Rings." I can still hear your little angelic voice. Exasperated, I'd stop the tape and we'd start all over again from the beginning...

....The birthday weekend at Joe's was easy, relaxing and fun—without my mother's monopolizing energy, I had a great time with my older brother and sister. But I missed Jon's presence and his energy.

I missed his quick wit and non-stop chatter while we played Dominoes; how he could either keep us in stitches laughing or held hostage...spellbound, with his long explanations of his point of view on just about any subject. He took after my Dad's brother Marty; a talker, for sure.

Jon often went golfing with Dad and my uncles, Marty and Lee, and he shared the story about the time when Marty was driving them to the course, one hand on the steering wheel and the other arm nonchalantly draped over the back of the front passenger seat, blabbering on while twisting and turning around to make eye contact with everyone in the car. Uncle Lee was riding shotgun, silently stewing, while Jon and Dad rode in the back, oblivious to Lee's burgeoning angst.

At one point in Marty's dissertation, Lee, who normally wouldn't say shit if he had a mouthful, explosively blurted out in his thick Maine accent, "FAH CHRIST'S SAKES MAH-TY, YAH SWERVIN ALL OVAH THA ROAD!"

Jon was a great impersonator and could parrot one of his favorite comics, George Carlin, with perfect timing. As a kid, he used to listen to his albums, had memorized many of his sketches and could recite them at random, especially the ones from the comic's early years. He'd do the radio disk jockey with all the sound effects; Monty Hall in the "Let's Make a Deal" skit imitating Carlin's rapid speech. *"...Ok...you have $500. What would you like to do? Keep the $500 or do you want to buy what Jay has in the box he's bringing down the aisle, Jay you wanna bring that box down.., Jay look out for the cord, Jay look out..BUD-DA-BUMP-BUMP... Okaay!... now we know what Jay had in the box...A cheeeese straightener...Deluxe model too..."* And Jon would keep us entertained for hours, reciting the whole album by heart.

He appreciated life's simplicity and had a strong connection to nature. He loved flowers as much as I do, so I would always text him photos of the first signs of spring...croci, daffodils and tulips popping up in Central Park, knowing how much he would enjoy them... and as I said, he had a great fondness for birds, sometimes to his detriment.

Years ago, he and Joe were visiting my dad in Florida and while walking through a parking lot, captivated by bird sounds and oblivious to what was in front of him, Jon walked straight into a metal trash can attached to a pole, injuring his leg and requiring a visit to the ER.

He could call in the birds by replicating their sounds and would spend hours sitting at his kitchen table, observing them visiting the feeders right outside the window, sharing with me the most minute details of their behaviors. I've never been that fascinated with birds but have grown to appreciate them through my brother's eyes and his love of them.

...At Joe's birthday gathering, we talked about Jon freely and I wept openly. Jan cried too but Joe was quiet and dry eyed. So, I asked him how he felt. Was he mourning Jon?

"No," he said. "Not anymore. Jon was my brother and my best friend and I have many memories to fall back on. I don't have any regrets."

He shared stories about their beloved men's sailing trips to
the Caribbean, cross country and downhill skiing in Maine, Jon's
old girlfriends…(I think he was fond of Debbie, and Jana had been
good for him except that she wanted children and Jon didn't)…
about the houses they built on Peaks Island…racing up to the top
of Mount Washington several times over, and I realized, Joe spent
much more time with Jon in the past 30 years, than I had.

At age 31, I left Maine and moved to New York City. Once,
while here on a visit, Jon met my friend Vicki. They hit it off
immediately, and after dating long distance for several months, he
moved down to live with her in New Jersey. Although preoccupied
and busy with our separate lives, we spent time together during
those few years he lived close by.

On one Thanksgiving, Jon, Vicki, my partner Chris
and I hosted dinner at my place in the City. We made all our
"traditional" foods and invited an eclectic group of friends. Jon
assembled his famous DiMauro relish dish made with anchovies,
olives, various hot peppers and celery and we cooked a turkey
with all the fixings.

I had a Kodak instant print camera and when the door
buzzer rang, I'd open it and Jon, standing next to me, snapped a
Polaroid, capturing our guests in that moment of surprise. We'd
hand over the picture to them. A silly souvenir of the day.

In the heat of summer, he and I would make a fast trip
back up to Maine on weekends. Jon would drive up on a Friday
night, we'd be at Scarborough beach, body surfing in the waves
on Saturday and then head back to the City Sunday night. It was
crazy. But we were young and didn't mind the long trip.

He spent a few years living with Vicki in New Jersey and
always wanted to continue to invest in real estate and his own
reconstruction properties. He put a bid on a house in Portland,
Maine and at the same time, applied for an entry level corporate
job in New York City, one that had opportunity for advancement

and upward mobility. The bid came through the same week he was offered the position in the City. He turned down the job and chose to move back to Maine.

At the time, being young, it didn't matter to me, but now, I sometimes regret that he left, and I often wonder what it would have been like for me, for us, if he had stayed here in New York. What experiences might we have shared? All the soul-searching work I was immersed in, maybe we could have journeyed through it together? Or knowing Jon's practicality, he might've considered it outrageous and frivolous to spend time and money on that.

"Too much navel gazing," I can hear him say.

Or would he have been open to it? Are we products of our environment? New York City energy has led me to explore personal growth and stretch comfort zones in a way I don't think I would have if I'd stayed in my provincial home town. I wonder if his life would have been different? And how Jon being here would have impacted my life? Two roads…we chose different paths.

My brothers had a full adult life together, living in close proximity, worked side by side in their own construction company and saw each other every day.

Maybe that's why Joe seemed more settled and at peace with Jon's death than I did. He had all their childhood AND adult history…memories of a lifetime together and had remained close right til the end of Jon's life. You'd think that would make his passing even more difficult. But Joe said he felt complete now, and I believed him. Or maybe it was the marijuana talking. He still grows his own…something they both enjoyed.

He said, "when Jon got sick, it broke my heart…and I wanted to be there for him…for Lisa… for whatever they needed."

And he was true to his word…arrived at their home every morning those first six months; assisted Jon physically out of the house and into the car, since he was too weak and unable to walk on his own, drove them to his treatments, sat by his side in the waiting room, doing puzzles together… and at one point, when Jon almost died from Neutropenia, (an abnormally low white blood cell count); a side effect of his Chemotherapy drug, Joe held his brother's hand while he received blood transfusions. And as Jon looked on with frightened eyes, his big brother cracked jokes and made small talk…in an effort to keep his spirits up…as well as his own.

My brother Joe taught me how to be around Jon, in his illness.

"Just stay positive and talk to him about everyday stuff. Don't keep asking him how he's feeling but let him tell you, if he wants to, and just listen. And don't get upset or cry in front of him, or show him your concern, fear or worry. Don't talk about anything heavy. Keep it light," he'd say.

Eventually the weekly blood transfusions worked and Jon's white blood cell count improved but he had to discontinue with the Chemo. He lost all his hair and, in solidarity, Joe wanted to shave his off too but his wife, Ursula, said no. Her brother was also sick with cancer. It would have been more than she could bear.

It was all so heartbreaking. Coincidentally, seven months into Jon's illness, Joe developed heart trouble and needed a pacemaker.

I think he had reached his tipping point…his heart was breaking too.

…Over the weekend, Jan, Joe and I discussed Jon's wife Lisa and shared our thoughts about their marriage and speculated on whether he was happy in it or not.

"They tussled." Joe said, simply, in his gentle unassuming way.

I sensed it at times, though Jon never let on to me about this. They were basically married but separated. She had moved upstate, close to her rented art studio and cared for her aging mother. They'd spend long weekends together every so often.

"He was torn up over it," my nephew Ryan revealed. He and Jon were confidants. More like brothers, than nephew and uncle, and would take off and spend days at Jon's remote oceanfront camp in Perry, Maine, just the two of them. Maybe it was the setting…surrounded by pristine nature with no sound for miles except the wind rustling through cedar trees and the gentle lapping of the sea at high tide that enabled Jon to drop his guard, expose his vulnerability and deepest truth with Ryan about his unhappiness in his marriage.

When Jon was in his early 20's, we lived together in the house he and Joe were renovating in South Portland. Jon's girl-friend of four years, Celeste, had ended their relationship and he was struggling to come to terms with the break up.

I was standing at the sink doing dishes, "how are you feeling today?" I asked him.

Unexpectedly he broke down and sobbed as he leaned into me for a consoling hug. I glanced at Joe over his shoulder and he looked concerned, embarrassed, not knowing what to do. Jon's young heart was breaking…he had been stoic, holding in his grief and it burst like a dam.

…"Lisa and I… our relationship has never been better," he'd say to me. "We talk for hours on the phone every day. It works best for us this way." Convincing himself what they had was enough. That he didn't need more.

I wondered if this may have contributed to his illness? The repressed feelings, the unexpressed grief…maybe feelings of loss and abandonment again? Only, this time in his marriage?… I can lie awake at night, ruminating on these useless reflections, but there's nothing I can or could have done about it. This was his journey, not mine. Marriage and finding a way to make things work in unconventional relationships is challenging. Jon was simple, practical and traditional in most regards, but also a non-conformist. And then to have to contend with a terminal illness on top of it all?

A therapist had once said to me, "When couples are confronted with these devastating challenges, they either fall together or they fall apart."

"I know I'm a burden to Lisa. I know how difficult this is for her," Jon blurted out to me in a weak and vulnerable moment.

I was grateful Lisa had come back home when Jon got sick but I'm angry it took him getting ill for that to happen. In my grief I want to blame her…blame someone. I know it's not fair and it's useless. And at times, I question if she came back out of love or out of a sense of obligation. Maybe both. Life and relationships are complicated.

I hope at the end of his life; he was able to trust in their love and feel nourished by it. I hope they fell together.

We all wanted to be there for him. I wanted to be there to the very end and told him so. To help him cross over. Hold his hand until Dad could take it on the other side, but he only chose Lisa to be present for his dying. I still struggle with his decision to die that way.

"He didn't want us to see him dying," Joe said. "Didn't want that to be our last image of him."

If that was true, it's typical of Jon—deciding on what he thinks is best for me. Maybe the truth is HE couldn't witness the reflection of our hearts in our eyes. Maybe it would have been too haunting, too painful an image for him to bear.

The last time I saw Jon, August 13, 2022

22

FUN IN THE SNOW & CLAIMS TO FAME

In winter, as youngsters during grammar school vacations, we'd wake up with eager anticipation, glance out the bedroom window hoping the weatherman had been correct in his storm prediction.

Yes! The world looked pure, untouched and pristine. Streets were covered in blankets, muffling the sounds of an occasional car creeping up the road on snow treaded tires. Snowbanks were piled high with fresh powder and tree branches hung low with heavy white shawls. A blizzard would still be raging but we didn't care; we were anxious to be the first ones out in it. Thick flakes would land on our eyelashes, and we'd stick out our tongues to catch a snow drink, trekking up to Larry Rowe's golf course for sledding.

We'd bring flying saucers and test out different hills, and once we found the perfect one, we'd slide down over and over, forging a trail. Sometimes we'd be the only ones out there, but as the day progressed, other neighborhood kids would show up and share our hill.

One trail was curved, just right, so we'd miss the tree at the bottom. We'd slide all morning until the twelve o'clock fire alarm would sound and then head home for lunch, take off soaking wet clothes and boots in the basement and drape them over the furnace to dry. I'd make Campbell's tomato soup with milk, and homemade croutons by cutting white bread into long strips and toasting them briefly in the oven on a cookie sheet.

We'd devour our lunch, go back to the basement, dig around for another complete set of dry clothing, and head back to the golf course for an afternoon of sliding. It had stopped snowing by now and the sun would be out. The trail was smooth, firmly packed down, and much faster now.

We'd return the following day, muscles and bones sore, battered from a day of sliding and bouncing hard on those aluminum flying saucers, but we loved it. The second day, even better, since the drop in temperature overnight would freeze the trail solid. We might take the sled or toboggan today but flying saucers were our favorites. We could fly down the hill now at top speed. Once dark, we'd trudge home, heavy in our completely soaked through clothing, exhausted and spent from another great day outdoors in the snow.

Sometimes we'd discover an ice patch and race home to get shovels, trade in our boots for skates, and wear them all the way back up, tiptoeing on skate cleats. We'd clear away the snow only to reveal a makeshift rink, full of bumps and divots. We didn't care. Bruised shins and tired ankles from skating in the cold for hours never seemed to bother us.

Joe, Jon and I would build snow forts out in front of the house and create a stockpile of snowballs to throw at passing cars or engage friends in snowball fights. When there was a big storm, and Mom and Dad were at work, we'd climb to the garage roof and practice aerial somersaulting off it into snowbanks piled high in the backyard. We'd do the same off the bulkhead roof in the summer onto an old mattress. Surprisingly, there were no serious neck injuries.

When Jon was seven, a classmate pushed him on the ice-skating rink out back of Thornton Heights School, and he fell and cracked his front tooth in half. Holding the bloody remainder of it in his hand, he walked in the back door, crying. Mom screamed and yelled in anger, and I got dizzy and nearly fainted.

In summer, Jon and I would often climb on the picket iron fence between our yard and the Shaw's, our next-door neighbors, and play Tarzan and Jane. We'd stand on the fence, leap and grab the tree branch in their yard, hang and swing from it.

"Depending on who's telling the story, I saved your life or if you're telling it, you saved mine. Ok, I'm telling it—this is how I remember.

I jumped and my arms safely latched onto the branch. As I was swinging from it, you attempted to do the same but one of your hands slipped and you started to fall. I quickly wrapped my legs around you in a scissor hold providing support, so you could reach up and securely grab a hold of the branch. Caught in the act again, we heard a loud wrapping on the window and Mr. Shaw yelling, "Get down from that tree!"

Jon, you once said a fantasy of yours was to be a rockstar. I thought the idea of fame was enticing to you, but it makes sense to me now.

"No one ever listens to me!" you would often complain in your need to be seen and heard and valued."

As kids, at home, we could never verbalize a complete thought —couldn't fully express an idea without being cut off, ignored or dismissed by adults, by our parents or by other siblings. We would either act out to get attention or clam up, isolate and shut down. Stop trying and give up. What's the use? There was no acknowledgement nor room for individuality. And we mimicked what we learned. Since WE had no voice, we didn't respect others when they were speaking. Never valued or were taught listening skills.

In my first acting class in New York City, the teacher assigned me a monologue. I memorized it by heart, knew it inside and out, but when I stood in front of the class, halfway through, I stopped cold. Self-conscious, tongue-tied, I couldn't go on. Not from sheer stage fright, but because it was awkward. New. Uncomfortable…noticing my classmates' silence…their undivided attention…listening to me without interrupting? I wasn't used to this. It was strange. People wanted to hear what I had to say?

Jon and I each had our brief moments of childhood fame reported in the local newspaper. On July 4th,1976 at the age of sixteen, he shot a hole in one on Larry Rowe's golf course and the Portland Press Herald wrote an article about him, complete with photo.

On the other hand, my infamous claim at ten years old—I had finished raking leaves, and piled them in the sewer drain in front of our house to burn. (It was common practice back then and everyone did this.)

I'd just lit the fire. BOOM! The manhole cover in the middle of the street popped up and cracked a strip of hardtop. Old nosey neighbor Emily Cushman came rushing out of her house and yelled at Jan, "put that fire out immediately! I'm calling the fire department!"

Apparently, the heat from the burning leaves ignited a leak in the gas main under the street. A reporter from the Press Herald came to interview me, asked me questions and quoted me, incorrectly…writing that I said, "the manhole cover jumped several feet off the ground." (I said inches.) My name appeared in the article entitled "Deafening Blast Rips Gas Main." Luckily, I didn't blow up the whole neighborhood.

23

SPIRITUALITY & VISITORS FROM BEYOND

David Kessler, one of the world's foremost experts on grief and loss said, "80% of people say they have had a sense that their bereaved are still around."

There are times, I've felt that my departed loved ones have come to visit me—to let me know they're watching over or maybe, just to say hello. Jon visits me in my dreams, and his spirit comes to me through birds.

In the last week of my Dad's life, I didn't get back to Maine to see him before he lost consciousness. Although it's said, even in a coma, the dying can still hear us, I felt guilty that I didn't make it there sooner. I arrived and he died a few hours later. I'm sure he waited for me.

But for months after I was wracked with guilt. Kicking myself for not getting to him sooner. Having regret for not doing enough. For one year after his death, I struggled with recurring bladder infections, something I never had before. Coincidentally my Dad died of bladder cancer.

I went to Diana, a channeler friend of mine, and as we all sat in a circle, she called in our spirit guides. I had a sudden strong sensation of someone standing behind me, felt the gentle comforting pressure of a hand on my back, and in a physical reaction to it, bowed forward, dropped my head and let go a well of tears and pain that had been bottled up inside me. It scared me and I went home to process it.

I spoke with Diana the next morning and I believe it was my Dad who came to console me and tell me everything's alright. That I did enough and to let go of my guilt. Soon thereafter, my bladder infections ceased.

One day as I was lost in thought, thinking about my father, I went into the Actors Federal Credit Union lobby, pressed the button for the elevator and said hello to the front desk attendant. He was an older man, with a pleasant demeanor, who had some similar qualities that reminded me of my Dad. He stepped into the elevator with me and started a conversation.

"Jeepers," he said, which stunned me because it was an expression my Dad often used. "I've got to pass water, and I can't seem to hold it as long anymore," he sheepishly confided.

I was touched by his vulnerability and as I walked out I smiled thinking to myself, *Well, hello to you too Dad. I love you and thanks for visiting*. I believe Spirit finds its way and speaks to us through others.

Years ago, I was in a long-term relationship with Chris and although it ended, I always felt a sense of safety and support from him. Whenever we took long road trips, he'd take on all the responsibility of driving while I sat in the passenger seat, dozing off. He was incredibly handy, stable and loyal, and when I'd get upset or cry, he'd intuitively know how to comfort me, by placing one hand on the back of my neck and the other on my forehead.

I had a dream last night in which I clearly heard Chris' voice say to me, *"Jo, I want you to come home."*

The words woke me up, and I felt myself smiling, feeling tranquil and rested. I believe his voice was my intuition, that small guide inside, that nudges me in the direction of my truth. "Home" symbolizing my authentic self.

When I was dancing in Sweet Charity's First National Touring Company, (which began in Toronto, June 1987), Bob Fosse died on our opening night in D.C. We had a brush up rehearsal with him in the afternoon, after which he headed back to his hotel to rest before the evening show. On his walk back to the theater with his wife Gwen Verdon, he dropped dead of a heart attack, unbeknownst to us at the time.

Craig, our stage manager, waited until after the show to call the whole cast and crew back on stage. We assumed we were going to get our early closing notice since ticket sales were waning. He said, "Bob died tonight."

"Bob who?" A cast member asked, thinking maybe he was referring to one of the hairdressers named Bob.

When Craig confirmed it was Fosse, several of us gasped and cried out in anguish, shock and disbelief. My friend Lynn fell to her knees. It couldn't be our Bob he was talking about? We had just spent all afternoon in rehearsal with him.

Once it registered, we were inconsolable, and for days after, many cast members shared experiences of sensing Bob's presence, or of him visiting them in dreams.

I went into a florist shop to buy some flowers for Gwen, and one of the workers pulled me aside feeling compelled to share his strange story with me.

Days earlier, while working in the shop, through the window, he saw a man fall down on the sidewalk who appeared to go unconscious, and as people started crowding around him, he could hear the man's voice in his own head talking to him, saying, *"I wish people would stop crowding me. Give me some space. I can't breathe with everyone hovering over me. I wish they'd just leave me alone and let me be."*

He had witnessed Bob's death through the shop window, not realizing that it was Bob Fosse dying, until he read about it in the papers the following day.

I relayed the florist's experience to the rest of the cast in the hope it might offer some comfort. Maybe Bob was trying to help us make sense of this tragedy and give us insight and understanding of what dying was like. So, we wouldn't be so afraid. That I happened to walk into the florist shop where I met and spoke with this stranger who witnessed his passing, seemed auspicious.

Ticket sales skyrocketed after the news broke and we closed to sold out houses in Boston. The irony. Death inspires appreciation and popularity.

We may think our dying loved one will attain wisdom and enlightenment as they get closer to death; that they will "know" how to die so we can take our cues from them, but the reality is they are experiencing something for the first time, something they've never been through before. It's all new and they're probably as clueless and as frightened as we are.

Or we think that someone who is dying is internally focused and completely self-concerned at the time of near death, which they have every right to be; but often that's not the case.

Rev. William Bergen of St. Ignatius Loyola shared a story of Fr. Lawrence Jenco, who visited his mother as she lay dying in a hospital. She tried speaking to him, but he couldn't make out what she was saying. As he bent down closer to hear her last words, assuming she wanted to convey something of deep meaning and insight to him, she clearly whispered, "Did you have lunch?" And then died within the hour.

A hospice worker who spent many hours with the dying had this advice. "Know your loved one. If they didn't like to be alone in life, they most likely won't want to be alone as they are passing. The opposite is also true. The same goes for physicality. If they were a toucher, then touch. If they weren't, please don't."

Maybe this is why Jon couldn't have us at his bedside when he was dying. He was not only protecting us, but he knew we would be a distraction for him on his final journey towards peace. I wonder if it's a jarring feeling like when you're drifting off to sleep and someone taps you on the shoulder?

Stephen Jenkinson states the only way to learn about death and dying is to spend more time around the dying, a shocking and disturbing suggestion, since fear of death is baked into our psyches as children and grows as we age. We run from the pain of it because as a culture, we're innately grief illiterate and death phobic. Our society is not versed in these teachings.

Perhaps, this is a necessary and viable concept to consider if we're to become more comfortable with endings. Trauma and grief tend to wait for us—they don't go away on their own and the mind replays what the heart cannot heal.

…It was a Sunday afternoon, summer 1970, I was sixteen. We had just arrived home, and my mother asked me to run to the store to pick up a Tab soda for her. Tab and Fresca were her special treats these days. I hopped on my bike and pedaled down the street to Gill's Pharmacy. My friend Karen's family owned the store and her father was the head pharmacist. We both worked there together at the front register after school and every other weekend day. I was off this Sunday.

I parked my bike out front and pulled on the front door to the store but it was locked. *That's strange,* I thought as I shrugged, turning around to get back on my bike to pedal home empty handed, Mrs. Ridell, (an employee), unlocked the door and called out to me.

"Joanne…Mr. Gill died today. He suffered a sudden heart attack while working and was taken away in an ambulance and died at the hospital…We've closed the store for the day."

I was in shock.

Karen was my best friend, lived three doors down from me on Keswick Road and I rode right by her house and went straight home to tell my parents. I didn't know what else to do and didn't want to intrude on their family's pain.

A short while later, Karen showed up at my back door. She didn't come in but stood on the steps outside and I opened the screen door and stood in the doorway, and we just looked at each other in disbelief.

"We're going to bury him in his brown suit," she flatly reported.

We were stilted and awkward. I don't think we hugged or shed tears or attempted to comfort each other. I didn't know death. Had no experience with it because no one I was close to had died. I didn't know how to be around death. How to feel about it. Or what to say to my best friend…

Most of us spend our lives keeping the fear of death at bay, and it may impact the extent to which we are able to embrace the present moment and be open to whatever today has to offer. Grief is an essential life skill that needs to be learned and passed down to the next generation. In some ways, Western culture is still very naive and primitive.

In 2012 I took a trip into the Amazon jungle and had the privilege of visiting with the Achuar, a deeply spiritual indigenous tribe, who are nicknamed "guardians of the rainforest." Our small group of seekers included nine women from the U.S. and Brazil and two local guides from Ecuador. We were welcomed into one family's dwelling, which consisted of a thatched roof hut with a dirt floor, no walls, a thin wooden bench that encircled the hut, some cooking utensils, minimal belongings, several hanging hammocks for sleeping and the remains of a makeshift fire in the center, used for cooking. We sat around drinking Chicha; the homemade beverage made of mashed yucca plant cooked and fermented with the enzymes from the spit of the woman preparing it. Since it would have been highly insulting to refuse the drink, I ignored my gag reflex and graciously accepted it. When in Rome…

I noticed a rough looking sarcophagus stone or cement structure in the corner of the hut and after much polite, three way translated questioning, from English to Spanish to Quechua and back again, we learned it housed their deceased Grandmother. That's how they roll here.

I caught my friend Kate's furtive glance as we pondered this revelation. To our sophisticated and critical Western thinking, this was bizarre. Cremation seems a more practical and palatable practice, and we can then either scatter or keep dear old Dad's ashes in an urn on the mantelpiece.

Or we bury our loved ones, far away from us in a cemetery, occasionally bring flowers and visit on special occasions, to momentarily commemorate them, and then return back to our lives and the living.

The Achuar believe, when they die, the soul still exists but the ancestors' spirit lives in an alternate realm. Out of reverence and respect for their deceased elder, they keep the remains of the departed loved one in the hut with them and continue to consult and include them in Dreamtime ceremonies and rituals.

Dreamtime is considered real time for the Achuar and must be examined and interpreted daily; for dreams are what give them insight, knowledge, guidance, and answers to all life decisions.

The relationship the Achuar maintain with their dead relatives seemed strange and foreign to me, and at first, primitive and morbid. But perhaps it's the opposite. Maybe they're advanced in their knowledge and understanding of states of consciousness and we're the naive ones.

I compare dying to birthing. We, as a society, have come full circle with birthing trends; from natural childbirth, to medicalized and controlled, now back to natural which is more accepted and considered a safer and healthier option for the mother and child.

I was with my friend Sonia for the birth of her son, Tomi. She was in pain for several months throughout her pregnancy and for weeks leading up to his birth. She asked if she could stay overnight at my apartment, when her labor pains began, since we lived closer to the hospital.

"Of course," I said and she and her husband Nuno, slept over on our sofa bed in the living room, snuck out in the middle of the night without waking us when her contractions intensified. We were asleep in the other room, and didn't hear a thing.

I got a phone call the next morning.

"Could you come by the hospital before going to work and drop off some pear nectar juice and fruit for me? Sonia asked. Maybe an egg sandwich for Nuno?"

"No problem," I said and when I arrived, I could see they were both distraught.

"Could you stay with me for an hour?" Sonia pleaded with frightened eyes.

"Sure." I said and I canceled my first client. After the hour came and went I could clearly see they needed me to stay so I canceled the rest of my morning clients and made myself available to them.

Her husband Nuno and I did our best to support Sonia. We took turns massaging her lower back, rocked her on a stability ball and chanted OM with her. I brought her food she could eat to keep her strength up and held her IV as she shuffled to the toilet in between screeching labor pains. Although in agony, and ludicrous as it seemed under the circumstances, she insisted I lay down strips of toilet paper on the seat before she sat down. I humored her and did what she wanted.

Birthing was scary, confusing, exhausting, messy and unpredictable. Her labor lasted for hours, and at one point, I went out for sandwiches and coffee for myself and Nuno. It was hard work and we needed sustenance too.

The room was an unsterilized mess, newspapers strewn about, trash from our food scraps, bags and clothing everywhere. Nuno and I were sticky in our street clothes, sneakers, jeans and sweatpants. No one was wearing hospital scrubs. It was nothing like I imagined it was supposed to be. I wasn't planning on being there for the birth but something or someone was calling me and asking this of me. Maybe it was her son's unborn spirit.

Then Tomi was ready to be born. Holy crap! Everything happened so quickly then. I hadn't even washed my hands. Sonia sat up and we each held one foot and encouraged her to push. It was excruciating for her and for us witnessing her pain and then it got better, busy, exciting, exhilarating yet still scary, and we were operating moment to moment, but it was beautiful and we were all overwhelmed and giddily crying with joy, relief and awe. Tomi came out with a WHOOSH like a little fish.

The doctor quickly stitched Sonia up, then vacated the premises. A nurse stepped in directing Nuno how to cut the umbilical cord, suctioned mucus from Tomi so his air passages would clear, then handed him off to us in the bassinet with instructions to keep "hitting" him, in order to stimulate his circulation, as his skin was somewhat bluish while she attended to Sonia. Nuno and I looked at each other perplexed, wondering, *how hard should we hit the little guy?* as we continued patting him down. Again, I hadn't washed my hands recently, but no one seemed to care.

Then mother and child were united at Sonia's breast, her parents arrived with little Clara, and everyone was ecstatic, cooing and ahhing over Tomi and the miracle that just occurred. And I snuggled her five-year-old daughter Clara in my lap, so sweet and shy, nervously giggling and beaming, excited to meet her new baby brother. From time to time, I tell Tomi his birth story and he rolls his eyes at me, as if to say, "who cares," oblivious to the awe and mystical wonder we all experienced with his arrival.

"For those who will fail to live forever, dying well is a right and responsibility of everyone. It is not a lifestyle option, but a moral, political, and spiritual obligation each person owes their ancestors and their heirs," writes Stephen Jenkinson.

Let's face it—none of us get out of here alive. Maybe it's time for us to learn to be present with dying in the same way we witness birthing, so we can accept death as a natural ending of our physical form on earth and perhaps even grow to understand and experience awe at the end of life too.

24

THE MOM EFFECT

There could be a correlation between the tumultuous relation-ship that existed between my mother and brother and his cancer; her overbearing influence and effect on him, (on all of us), could have been a contributing factor.

Jon was an empath and highly sensitive person. *The Problem* section of the *Big Red Book of Adult Children of Alcoholics and Dysfunctional Families*, states that *"How we were infected as children continues to affect us today as adults."* And if we have no place to process, release and properly grieve our childhood wounds and life traumas, they can become embedded in the body, create energy blockages, and over time manifest as derangement and disease, suggests Dr. Samuel Hahnemann, founder of the Homeopathic System of Medicine.

Kelly Turner, Ph.D., researcher and psychotherapist spe-cializing in Integrative Oncology, looks at thousands of cases of cancer remission and identifies the nine key factors survivors have in common, in her book *Radical Remission, Surviving Cancer at All Odds.* She discusses the correlation between suppressed emotions and cancer.

Dr. Tsuneo Kobayashi, an integrative oncologist in Tokyo, believes cancer cells are "merely healthy cells whose mitochondria have become damaged, and suppressing emotions is one of the key elements that can damage mitochondria."

My Mom and Dad were children having children, carrying their own repressed emotions and childhood traumas with them into adulthood, as did their parents before them. Generational dysfunction. Raising a family of four children by the age of 30, they did the best they could with limited resources. It's not their fault nor do I blame them.

They were always fighting, my Mom and Dad…screaming matches…hitting…streaks of coffee stains on the kitchen cabinets from my mother hurling her cup of hot coffee across the room at my Dad…and scads of tears, (my Mom's and our own). After an episode, things would be volatile and tense for days and we walked around on tiptoe, praying for resolution.

"When I leave your Dad, do you want to live with him or me?" my Mom sobbed as we sped off in the car. She'd confide in me, too much for my adolescent ears; as if I could play therapist, while she gathered her motives, deciding on how to leave him.

"I want to stay with you," I blurted out. Feeling a *"Sophie's Choice"* sickness with having to choose, but less painful than the silence of her contempt if I answered otherwise. I was loyal to her. My fear and anxiety increased my need to cling to her even though my source of comfort was also my source of terror.

The next day, everything would be back to "normal." No explanation to any of us. Not even a "we're sorry we scared you." We didn't talk about it, fearing it might bring on another episode.

…A birthday ritual at our house was Betty Crocker's angel food cake. I was blending the ingredients using the electric hand mixers. Six-year-old Jon, kneeling on a stool at the kitchen bar so he could peek over the bowl at what I was doing, anxiously waited for me to finish. His special treat was licking the batter off the beaters. When I stuck a knife in the bowl to scrape the sides it caused a spurt of cake mix to launch directly into Jon's eye. I rinsed it out as best I could but the following morning he woke up with a puffy eye, swollen shut.

It was Saturday, my Dad's only day of the week free of us, to do what he cherished—spend the morning golfing. But with one car to the household, he was obligated to drive Jon to the ER instead. I went with them.

We sat for hours, waiting. Dad, jingling loose change in his pockets, paced up and down the corridor, his T-off time fast approaching. At one point he spotted a policeman in the emergency waiting room and urged me, "Go ask that officer if he'll give you a ride home, when Jon's done with the doctor."

"Daad!... I'm not going to do that!" I scolded. How dare he ask that of me! My Dad, self-absorbed and distant at times, was emotionally unavailable and I didn't understand him. Wasn't he concerned for Jon? For me? I felt like we'd switched roles, (I was the parent and he was the child). He was detached and it frightened me. As if he could walk away and leave us without looking back.

Maybe we were all too much for him. Golf was his saving grace and the only escape away from the burdens of marriage and family life. He wanted two children, but my mother insisted on four.

"Every one of you was planned," my Mom would say. I was child number three. Jon came four years later, a delightful gift for my Dad and they developed a special bond and closeness. Maybe because my father was older; mature enough at that point to enjoy fatherhood.

My father seemed disinterested in me. But we wrote letters when I was away at college. We carried on our own private correspondence. Just the two of us. He tried to have a relationship with me, but my mother prevented it by needing to be included in everything and my Dad always deferred to her. He loved her and it was too emotionally exhausting for him to do otherwise.

On our family trips to Boston, my Dad would say, "Thank you sir," as he took the ticket from the Maine Turnpike toll booth attendant. This irked my mother, for some reason, and she would belittle my father for addressing the worker with respect. Often criticizing and shaming my Dad in front of us, I modeled her behavior and as a result, I too was ashamed of my father.

Another birthday ritual: we'd go out to dinner with Mom and Dad on our special day. Just us three without siblings, to Valle's Steak House, (the only game in town back then in the 60's). I would have preferred my brothers and sister with me for camaraderie and support. Mom would be throwing verbal hate daggers at Dad all during dinner and then her alter ego would suddenly appear and sweetly ask me across the table, "How's your steak honey?"

In my late teens and early 20's I couldn't eat in restaurants without breaking out in a cold sweat, nausea welling up in my throat at the smell and sight of food and I'd spend most of the time sick in the bathroom. I couldn't keep any food down. Fortunately, I outgrew it.

I pitied my Dad because my mother consistently reprimanded him. I loved him. Didn't understand him but felt proud and sorry for him at the same time. Looking back now, I recognize this was the source of my character trait of confusing love with pity.

He was dependable, consistent and I could count on him to show up when he said he would. He'd be there at 5:20 on the dot to pick me up from Dorothy Mason's School of Dance after my tap class, unlike my mother who could keep me waiting for an hour without explanation.

"What?" she'd ask. As if nothing was out of the ordinary and I was the crazy one for being miffed.

Dad played Twister with us and wiffle ball in the backyard after supper. I can still hear him howling with laughter as we'd tag him out running the bases, tackling him to the ground and all of us piling on top of him.

My poor mother, a tormented soul, was the opposite and expected us to fulfill her emotional needs and soothe her inner turmoil. We all fled the house as soon as we were old enough. Jon, being the youngest, and the last one to leave home inherited liaison patrol duty for my parents' dysfunctional relationship. The emotional toll was enormous.

Disagreeing with my mother was not tolerated. Showing anger was unacceptable. We were trained to be obedient little foot soldiers. Particularly Jon. He was the "good" son. Never acted out or complained about his role. Our main chore was to make sure Mom was happy. Jon enlisted full time.

I think of my Mom as a cross between Joan Crawford in *Mommy Dearest* and Francis McDormand's character as *Olive Kitteridge*. Fun, beautiful, emotionally volatile, manipulative, controlling, unhappy, and often sickly, but at the same time tough as nails. A survivor, yet helpless, needy and narcissistic. Cruelty and tenderness in combination.

"Take me to zee kasbah!" she'd play, while kissing and snuggling me in her arms. I was intrigued. What was "a kasbah?" Invoking images in my childish mind of an exotic place, nuns shuffling around wearing full black and white habits, speaking in hushed tones. Wrong religion. But regardless, an image had been permanently implanted. (I still desire to visit a Moroccan kasbah).

And she was creative. We'd make festive decorations and crafts for each holiday. In her artist smock and jeans with a triangle kerchief to keep her hair back, she'd drive me around in search of wild holly, flowering weeds, and cat-o-nine tails. When spotted roadside, she'd pull over and pass me the scissors to get out and collect them. We'd gather pinecones, acorns and evergreen branches and bring them back home to her workbench in the cellar and I'd assist her, creating swags and wreaths to decorate the house for Christmas.

But without warning, she could snap like a pit bull, and her mood would swing like Jekyll and Hyde. Her rage was scary. Never knowing what new incident would ignite her, we were left balancing ourselves on the tightrope of her emotions.

Although, according to my mother, "I wanted each and every one of you," in a fit of rage she'd scream, "if I had it to do all over again, I wouldn't have had any of you!"

But she could be fun, too. That's what was confusing. We'd play "monster." She'd shut off all the lights and slowly stomp around upstairs, and in a dark throaty voice say, "I'm gonna find you and GET you!" We'd giggle and squeal in nervous delight, hide underneath her bed, all squished together in the center so she couldn't reach us. She'd pounce on top of the bed, and we'd get so worked up and spooked, inevitably one of us would end up crying. Lights would switch on, game over and Mom would hug and soothe whomever it was who was crying; usually Jon or me.

And she could be emotionally available, thriving on remedying our problems. "What's wrong? Sit and tell me about it." She'd be lying on her bed and I'd open the squeaky sliding closet door across from her, move my Dad's shoes and clothes aside to make room, sit on the ledge, and bare my soul as I sat in the midst of the faint stale odor of my Dad's suit jackets and shirts, surrounding me with his silent comforting, as she'd listen intently to my saga.

When Jon got sick with cancer, I gave him Kelly Turner's book, Radical Remission, and he embraced it. He implemented all nine factors, utilizing them diligently, working towards releasing his suppressed emotions. As a result, my brother and Lisa chose to limit their contact with family members, specifically ending all contact with my mother. They believed she was too emotionally toxic, and they didn't have the capacity for exposure to her energy anymore.

Jon needed to do this—for his own survival. He was disabled and unable to work, and Lisa was his full-time caregiver. They depended on my mother's financial support for their livelihood. And she generously provided it, though at times, employed manipulative tactics, threatening to cut back or stop it altogether if her wants and needs were not met. She would pressure all of us to try and convince Jon to see her. In particular, she'd pressure Joe.

It was extremely difficult dealing with my mother throughout the 46 months of Jon's illness; her incessant needs and hysterical demands on all of us and her inability to understand and honor Jon's wishes were overwhelming. All our lives we'd been made to feel responsible for her emotional needs and this was, by far, our biggest challenge yet.

Navigating Jon's decision to isolate from her was a huge challenge. We wanted to support him in whatever he felt he needed for his own survival, but at the same time it created a huge chasm in the family.

"I don't understand it! She's his mother after all, and is supporting them," Joe would say in earnest, bewildered that Jon could cut her out like this. Bruno and his family also couldn't understand why a son cannot speak with his mother. Most people don't get it.

Even I caved under the pressure. Once. She fell and broke her wrist and begged to see Jon, 'before she died" so I went to Maine and set up a Facetime call for them. Big mistake. Like a drug addict, it only whet her appetite. Dissatisfying for my mother and infuriating for Jon. She recovered from her fall and lived on, strong as ever.

I'm sorry Jon.

At the time, Jon and Lisa's decision was troubling me as well because I was entangled in family dysfunction and enabling. Taking daily phone calls from my mother, attempting to comfort her, to make my brother's terminal illness and his choices palatable, trying to soothe her with anything I could muster to soften the reality that Jon wanted nothing more to do with her, yet accept her financial support, drained my emotional energy. I felt hollow and spent. Battling with my pain and anger, my grief and inability to cope, to understand, to process all this and make sense of his tragedy was insurmountable. Learning how to salvage my feelings and my family's grief over Jon was a relentless struggle. We were a family enmeshed in everyone else's business, under the guise of love. It was exhausting separating and allowing space for my feelings without becoming immersed and pummeled by the family tide.

And my grief over Jon was unearthing my own buried traumas of the past. I needed to seek outside help and support to heal these old wounds. We all needed help.

I had a dream. I was upset about Jon and his health, his estranged relationship with my mother and the family dysfunction. He was dressed all in black, hugging me and reassuring me that all would be resolved and he would take care of everything.

I woke up - a) feeling disturbed that he was cloaked in black and, b) recognizing the dream was a premonition. A message from Jon. He was right. I couldn't have imagined things would turn out the way they have. Sometimes death is a rupture, an opening, a window through which we all can heal.

My job in the family had always been the fixer, the peacemaker, and I want to relinquish that role now. Jon's dying forced me into retirement.

Joe has since stepped in, as replacement for Jon, as my mother's caretaker and confidant. Saint Joe. Maybe his false sense of guilt, from being the rebellious troubled teen, motivates him to be so forgiving and obedient to her.

…He ran away from home at sixteen; jumped on a freight train to Boston. It was late and he hadn't returned home from his part time job that evening. We called everyone—had they seen Joey? No one had. I searched the neighborhood in a torrential rainstorm, soaking wet, crying out, "JO-EEEEE!" thinking he could be hiding somewhere or hurt and would hear me above the fray of the storm. It was senseless.

My Mom needed tranquilizers. We were fraught with despair, imagining the worst, and no one slept a wink that night. The next morning a New Hampshire state trooper called. They had picked up Joey hitchhiking on the Maine Turnpike heading north—heading home. Could we come get him?

My Mom and Dad drove to New Hampshire, brought him back and the three of them spent time alone in his room, talking quietly. With ears pressed against the closed door, Jan, Jon and I tried to decipher what was being said.

The door opened. No one spoke to us. Nothing was shared. The shame overshadowed the need from our questioning eyes. What happened? We wanted answers, reassurance, comfort. I cried and hugged Joey but that was all. We never spoke of it again. Another family secret tucked away, weighing heavy on our hearts…

I'm curious about indigenous tribes, like the Achuar in the Amazon; how they handle family tragedies as a community and accept loss, dying and death simply as stages of life. Public grieving: mourning and wailing together as a community and going off alone when needed, are customary.

Western culture values independence, privacy and stoicism in these matters. I attended a friend's funeral service at Central Synagogue. Properly dressed mourners demurely dabbed tissues at their nose and eyes and not a sound was heard coming from anyone except the speaker. Public display of grief is socially unacceptable and could be considered a sign of weakness. "Pull it together!" …"Oh, she's a wreck!" …*And why wouldn't she be?*

This Western behavior seems counterproductive. Stifling. How can suppression of deep sadness and loss be healthy?

25

DEATH IS MY TEACHER

"Death is a great teacher, but who lives with that level of awareness? What are you doing with your life? That is what death asks you," says Michael Singer in *The Untethered Soul*.

Long before he ever got sick, Jon and I would often play the game of reflecting on the question, *"If you knew you were going to die in a month, how would you live your life today?"* As a kid, I would answer emphatically, "I'd buy grape juice and drink it straight without diluting it with water... (frustrated that my Dad always did this to stretch groceries to last the week). "And I'd buy full strength chocolate milk already made, in the glass bottle instead of Nestle's Quik." It seemed daring and extravagant.

When I was older, I'd answer, "Quit my job and take off traveling to distant lands and experience different cultures." I thought I needed that to feel I had lived.

Jon said, "I would do nothing different. I feel excited and happy to be alive. Everyday I'm here is a blessing. I just want to enjoy being present, right here, right now and appreciate all that life has to offer me."

It didn't take dying to challenge Jon to live at his highest level. He was living his life truly awakened from the deepest part of himself.

It took his dying for me to discover my deepest truths and what really matters.

I cut off my long thick curly hair in January after his death and have decided to keep it short, straight and let it go naturally gray. Death of a close loved one shifts priorities and what was so important before, seems trivial and superficial now.

It's winter and I'm noticing how dry I feel. Especially my scalp. Not sure if it's the time of year or the haircut but I wake up at night feeling my scalp—painful, dry, itchy, and very sore to the touch. Feels like I have a vise-grip on my scalp and I immediately think of Jon. How he must have felt all those 3 ½ years, day in and day out wearing that Optune device. How could he tolerate it? There must have been times when he wanted to scream and yank that thing off.

I wake up in a panic that I can't get away from this feeling on my scalp. It makes me anxious and I imagine what Jon had to go through. What he had to endure. What he CHOSE to endure. So he could have "more time." I have respect and admiration for him but not his courage.

…Jon's Optune head device had to be changed every three days. It was a process. He would unhook the Optune device from the electrical unit and strip off the arrays that were taped to his scalp. Lisa (or me, when I was caretaking), would wash his scalp and shave his head making sure to remove all stubble and leave it as smooth as possible. Lisa would use a straight edge with shaving cream, but I didn't dare. I wasn't as confident and was afraid I'd cut his scalp, so I'd use the electric razor.

Once his head was shaved as close and smooth as possible, I'd spray alcohol and massage his exposed scalp, giving him a much-needed break from the restricted head device. I enjoyed this part. The closeness. Being able to gently touch his scalp and provide brief moments of comfort. I think he did too. Who doesn't enjoy a head massage?

…When Jon was little, I often had the job of washing his hair in our bathroom sink. He'd lean over the counter as I shampooed him, and in my effort to clean and rinse out his hair, I accidently bumped his head on the faucet.

"That's one time," he'd count at me.

"Sorry, I didn't mean to." The sink was tiny. I was doing the best I could.

"That's two," he'd complain again.

"THREE, FOUR, FIVE!" I'd purposely bump his head, infuriated with this chore that had been delegated to me.

I'm sorry Jon…

…After the shave and massage, he'd sit relaxing in the kitchen for a while, breathing in the freedom of no Optune while I'd prepare a new set of arrays for re-application. They needed to be placed strategically, different from the placement of the previous set, so as to cover the complete brain territory to prevent tumor regrowth. Lisa had drawn designs of where to place them on alternating charts, so I'd know how to do it when she was away.

It was stressful. I was worried I'd put them in the wrong positions, permitting his cancer to take hold and grow again or I'd cause scalp sores and burns from the arrays.

Once cut, trimmed and adhered to their respective spots on his head, I'd thread through the electrical cords and plug them into the proper outlet on the device. That device would go off occasionally in the middle of the night, beep beep beeping, like the sound of a truck backing up, if the cords loosened or were plugged in incorrectly. It was aggravating…

Early on he was asked to be a lead speaker in a Cancer support group, to share his experience with using the Optune device on a Zoom meeting with a therapist and some new cancer patients. I was with him, (off camera), and as is typical, once Jon starts speaking about something he's passionate and confident about, there's no stopping him.

He digressed from the Optune into touting the virtues of the nine key factors outlined in the book, *Radical Remission, Surviving Cancer Against All Odds*. Without even seeing the screen, I could "read" the room and sensed these folks, (newbies to the cancer world), listening to him with bug-eyed stares. Like deer in the headlights, overwhelmed, unfamiliar with the concepts Jon was rambling on about, as he spoke graduate level language to kindergarteners.

Reminded me of a former therapist demonstrating my forced attempts to get my partner, Chris, to accept and join in my newfound realizations.

"This is you, " she simulated shoving a pie in my face. "Here's the pie. It's delicious! Eat it, it's good! Go ahead and eat it! You'll love it."

She suggested I might try a gentler less forceful tactic to share my process work.

Jon and I shared our enthusiasm to help others. Sometimes too much.

<h1 style="text-align:center">26</h1>

BREAKDOWNS IN COMMUNICATION

October 6, 2023

I'm 68 and I still feel scared to set boundaries with your mother, can you believe it Jon? I'm flying to Maine today and have that usual pit in my stomach. A slightly nauseous feeling that comes over me when I'm returning home. Like I'm heading into the lion's den. Usually, Bruno is with me as a buffer, but this time I'm going alone, emotionally naked.

Mom is 93, a little old woman now but still feisty and fiery and as emotionally needy as ever. That hasn't seemed to dissipate at all with age.

And your sister Jan too, whose relationship with Mom…well, you know. I'm just realizing Mom's desire for me to come for this visit may be so I can act as the go-between, the peacemaker between them; to assume my old familiar family role. She doesn't just want to see me, but wants me to be of service to her with her problems with Jan.

What would it feel like to let go of that job? Frightening. Terrifying. If I lean into my powerlessness, my inability to change or fix them and their relationship, I'm nothing. My family obligation will be taken away so then what is my purpose? Who am I without it?

That old feeling of not feeling safe, as if the floor beneath me is collapsing returns now. Who's going to catch and support me if I fail to fix them?

But intellectually my adult self knows better. I'm not nine years old with a raging mother who is out of control. I am my own loving support. I can see my mother and sister with all their personal struggles and stories and step back and remain a silent witness. Breathe, stay with and comfort my inner child and not enter the drama triangle.

I have real lucid moments when I know I'm ok and trust they'll be ok too. I can let go of this job and turn it over to a higher consciousness and intentionally focus on joy and love for myself, and for Jon, now completely healed and whole and blessed.

I'm doing well, most of the time. Living my life full out, feeling happy, joyous and free, and when people ask me about Jon, I can talk about him now without breaking down. Sometimes… But for the past few weeks I haven't been able to sleep through the night and nothing I usually do is working.

Because I am a delayed feeler, it takes me a day or so to recognize, acknowledge and identify what I'm feeling. I realize I've been disassociating from my grief. Trying not to think about the sadness and the loss. *I miss you Jon. I miss your energetic presence here on earth.*

Someone shared in a meeting the other day and it triggered me. It hit me again like a Tsunami and the flood gates opened and I felt raw grief again. I need to make room for my grief and not bury it. Allow it space and breathing room. Today I feel better. The dam cracked and I shared.

I'm not putting away my Jon altar or cleaning things up yet. I don't want to. It doesn't feel right.

December 22, 2023

In the spirit of Christmas, I sent Lisa a card saying, *"you're always in my heart and I wish you peace, love and healing."* I received the card back in the mail today, unopened with a handwritten index card from her stating: *"I must ask you to respect my firm boundary. I want no further contact from any member of your family. Interacting is destructive to my health. Please accept this is exactly how it was meant to be. It is over. My health will not allow it. I wish you all peace and good lives. I have closed this book. Regret nothing. Jon is free. Please let me go."*

Stunned, I felt punched in the stomach. I struggled to understand her…*Weren't we close? We'd been through so much and we could help and support each other in our grief. After all we've been through together? …*

She emailed me after Jon passed, expressing her need of at least two years of no contact with any of us to heal. It's been sixteen months so, technically, I hadn't honored her wishes, but this was so final…. *No further contact….* Everyone handles grief differently and I must respect her need for complete detachment, remembering she operated best in the extremes. But this? …

…After 35 years of a tumultuous marriage, my mother and father divorced. My Dad immediately moved to Florida and only came back north to spend summers in Maine. So for 18 years, unless we traveled to Florida to visit him, we would only see him during those three months in the summertime. Jon would go down to Florida about every few years, when he could, to spend a week or two visiting and golfing with Dad. They had the closest relationship of any of us.

We'd only speak occasionally on birthdays and holidays. "Hi Joni!" my Dad would always say in that upbeat way of his, once he recognized it was me on the phone. He was the only one who still called me Joni, my nickname from childhood.

He was never much of a communicator. Our phone conversations were light. Nothing too personal. We talked briefly about the weather, about food. He really loved to eat and often an event would be measured by how "unreal" or "out of this world" the food was. Two of his favorite expressions.

…It was 2004. My Dad, at 79, was now living in Sarasota, Florida in his girlfriend's home and struggling with a new developing health concern, possibly bladder cancer. Jon and Joe had just come back from staying with them for a week and expressed their concern over my Dad's relationship with Clara and his looming health issue. It sounded like an unmanageable situation so I felt compelled to go down there and see what was going on and if I could be of any help.

It was a torrential rainstorm when Dad picked me up at the airport in his small grey sedan packed to the gills with his personal belongings. The front passenger seat was pushed so far forward to accommodate all the contents of the car, I could barely squeeze into it without having to lean on the dashboard.

Sticking out in the backseat on top of piles of clothes and all my Dad's things was the metal golfer mailbox bracket that had hung on our mailbox at Keswick Road, the old homestead. We had given it to him one year for Father's Day. I was touched. After all these years he had kept that one memento of our life together back then.

"Dad, what's going on?" I nonchalantly asked as I wedged myself into the front seat. "What's with all this stuff?"

"Oh, Clara and I are not getting along. She's not speaking to me and wants me to move out. So, I'm going to head to the East Coast of Florida to stay with a friend." By friend, he meant his other girlfriend. He had been spending summers in Maine without Clara, and while in Maine he'd met another woman, Claire, who also summered in Maine but wintered on the opposite coast of Florida. Though he liked having a woman in his life, after being tied down in two consecutive long marriages, he enjoyed his freedom and non-committal bachelorhood. No grass grew under his feet. He was a minimalist nomad, with few personal belongings, and had no problem moving from place to place.

"Did she invite you to stay with her? And does she know you're coming and bringing all your things with you?"

"No. I was going to show up and stay at a hotel and let her know I'm in town."

"Okaay…maybe not so fast Dad. You can't just show up and expect her to take you in." I gently suggested. "Don't you think you should call her first and let her know what you're planning on doing?"

Although he was outwardly unemotional, I could sense my father's desperation, and I wanted to help him. Women had been taking care of him for so long, he knew no other way.

"But first things first. Let's go to the doctor's together and find out what's going on with your bladder," I said. "I'd like to hear it directly from him."

Clara's house was a hoarder's collection of knickknacks, tchotchkes and tacky art shell furniture. My Dad was assigned the use of the outside bathroom and shower only, since the inside one was hers; full of nylon stockings and hand washables draped over the shower rod and wooden clothes rack, cluttered with more tchotchkes and wall fixtures, and with barely any room to maneuver, without knocking something over.

Her car pulled into the driveway.

Clara was attractive, warm and congenial. She suggested we three go out for dinner.

Dinner was superficially pleasant. Clara and I made small talk while Dad remained silent. After dinner we came back and sat down at the kitchen table to discuss what was going on. My dad's health problems, their relationship. I played therapist.

Big breakdown in communication. Apparently, my Dad had given Clara a ring which she mistook for an engagement ring and assumed they'd get married, she'd be able to quit work, and my father would provide her with financial support.

My Dad had no intention of marrying again nor sharing his retirement pension.

Angry and disappointed, Clara had stopped talking to my father and asked him to move out. This was a deal breaker for her.

I tried to convey to them how their misunderstanding had hurt them both. I empathized and could see they still cared for one another. So, I encouraged them to look each other in the eye as they spoke instead of looking at me and speaking through me.

I spoke for my Dad and asked Clara for more time for him.

"Could you give him that?"

"Yes," she replied.

Deescalating the conflict. For now, anyway. I got busy focusing on solutions. I was there for three more days, and it was pouring rain the whole time. So much for sunny Florida.

I looked through the local newspaper for apartment rentals for Dad. We met with his doctor and attended a convention with various seminars on cancer treatments, to explore options.

We visited the funeral home, where he had bought and paid for a complete package of services, to see if we could transfer it to a sister funeral home in Maine, close to family. We could and we did.

One night Clara talked to me privately. Dad had gone to bed early.

"I think your father is losing his mind. I think the cancer is affecting his brain."

"How so?"

"I try to discuss things with him, and he acts like he doesn't comprehend or know what I'm talking about."

I was concerned, so once alone, with my Dad, I asked him about this.

"I hear everything and understand what she says," he assured me. "I just tune her out and let her talk. It's easier for me than getting into an argument with her."

I wonder if that's a family trait, a coping mechanism passed down from my father to my brother Jon. Maybe it was easier for him too. Relent, rather than arguing with Lisa.

Jon was trapped between our family's overbearing love and concern for him and Lisa's wants and needs. He had decided on what would give him the most amount of peace and serenity, allowing him to devote his dwindling energy and focus solely on his healing. And he chose Lisa to be his primary caretaker, made the decision to pull away from family members when he became ill, limiting his time with us, cutting us off completely in the final weeks of his life. Did he do that for himself? Or did he do it for Lisa? Maybe it was more convenient for him to do what she wanted (and of course, that was his prerogative—if that made his ending easier). I hope his decisions were his heart's truth.

…In 2009, Dad was in Maine for the summer, and as usual, staying in Joe's other apartment house in Portland, in a third-floor makeshift unit without a kitchen. It had worked for him for his brief summer stays since he spent much of his time golfing, out at his girlfriend's and busy socializing. But now his cancer had progressed to the point where this was no longer appropriate. We needed to get him set up in a proper apartment, realizing that he would not be going back to Florida in the fall. His health wouldn't allow for him to live far from family at this point. But my Dad was in denial.

"Oh, I'm sure I'll be fine by the fall and be able to winter in Florida."

We didn't want to upset him so we avoided discussing it. He was under the care of an excellent local urologist now, but he was unable to give my Dad a definitive explanation of how long he could maintain a good quality of life nor an accurate prognosis.

We found an apartment conveniently close to my sister's house and set it up with a new comfortable bed and furniture. Lisa found a great second-hand Lazy Boy that he could sit in, kick back and listen to his country western music on recorded tapes he had made. The Griffin Club was down the street, close enough to walk to, where he could watch his beloved Red Sox on TV, sit at the bar drinking orange juice and socialize with friends.

When we brought Dad over to the apartment for the first time, his voice quaked and he choked back tears, "You did all this for me?"

Having graduated from the Institute for Integrative Nutrition, I was on a mission to save my father with natural medicine. I learned about all the foods and supplements that could address his condition and fervently made diet plans for him, with the help of my siblings and sister-in-law, Lisa. They'd cook for him, prepare healthy meals for the week and stock his freezer. Whenever I'd be in Maine visiting, I'd cook for him and make green super food smoothies. I was determined to heal him.

He was still living independently, doing the things he loved; golfing, socializing, loving, laughing, playing his guitar and enjoying every moment and he kept his declining health a secret from us. I arrived one day, after driving up from New York City, stepped into his bathroom, and found blood everywhere in and around the toilet.

"What happened Dad?! What's going on with you?" I was alarmed. We sat down and had a heart to heart.

"I'm passing blood clots in my urine now and sometimes I can't pee because it feels blocked. And jeepers, I don't have enough energy anymore to walk down the street to the store."

I informed my siblings that things were seriously changing with Dad. We immediately made a doctor's appointment and I went with him.

Dr. Broadus had recently completed a last resort, bladder wash treatment on him and after tests and further examination reported, matter of factly, "the cancer has spread outside the bladder and there is nothing more that can be done to treat it."

Stunned, my Dad and I walked out of the office and stood in the stairwell, looking at each other in shock and disbelief.

"I guess this is the end of the line, Joni."

I broke down crying and hugged my father as we wept together, our sobs echoing in the stairwell.

My brothers, sister and I got busy looking for assisted living places and nursing homes that could possibly take him in immediately because it was clear he wouldn't be able to live independently much longer.

Days later with things still unsettled, I reluctantly left to go back to New York City.

"Dad, if you can't urinate, it's very dangerous and you MUST call 911 to go to the emergency room immediately," I was emphatic.

And as was predicted, days after I left, blood clots formed and unable to urinate, my father was rushed to the ER. Dad was admitted to the hospital for a one week stay and the Foley Catheter was the only thing that kept him free of pain and his bladder unblocked.

My brother Joe was at his hospital bedside daily, conferring with the doctors and discussing plans for what were his next options. Jon was away upstate with Lisa, working a craft show.

We were fraught with what to do with my father. How would we manage this? He needed full time care. Finding a facility that would operate a Foley Catheter was next to impossible. My sister and I visited a nursing home and felt sick about it. He didn't belong there, nor did they have the equipment to keep him alive anyway. What other choices did we have?

Dad was released from the hospital after a week and my brother Joe generously took him into his home under Hospice Care. Saint Joe. It was an exhausting ordeal for Joe and his wife Ursula. Without around the clock care, sleep was fleeting.

Dad was on morphine now and would increasingly become agitated and hallucinate. As soon as Joe tried to go to bed himself, Dad would attempt to get out of bed, "I need to get to the golf course for T-off time," he'd anguish.

Joe had to forcibly lay him back down, feeling a mixture of impatience, guilt and remorse—overwhelmed and weary from limited help and lack of sleep.

By the middle of the second week in the comforting care of Joe's home, my Dad slipped into a coma. Friday of that week, his end was near. The family gathered and sat in vigilance at my father's bedside. We laid our hands on his body and my brother Joe said, "We're all here Dad and we love you. It's okay. You can go now. Put in a good word for me up there, wouldja, cause God knows I'll need it."

And my father took his final breath and let go.

I was irritated with my Mom. She injured herself again and is resistant about hiring more home health aides. Not that she can't afford it…Depression era mentality runs deep.

Her phone calls interrupted me several times while I was playing tennis tonight but since I was on the court, mid-game, once I recognized the number, I ignored the incessant ringing. I'd call her back later.

I didn't play well and my knee was bothering me. I was feeling l'uovo torto, as Bruno would say, (an Italian expression meaning "disagreeable; irritable"). With a chip on my shoulder, I returned her phone call.

As usual the television was on volume 15 in the background. She couldn't hear me and God knows why it never occurs to her to lower the volume when she gets on the phone.

She was insistent on making her point about something and like fingernails on a chalkboard started ranting, "YOU'RE NOT LISTENING TO ME!" obstinately repeating herself and "LET ME FINISH!" Two of her favorite phrases. Bruno says we need to make her a t-shirt printed in bold letters "LET ME FINISH!"

Granted, she's 93 and it's hard to tell on the phone when someone's done talking and it's your turn to speak. We tend to talk over each other at the same time. Jon tried once to implement the walkie talkie tool of "over"—signaling to me when he was finished talking and the cue for me to start my share. It was innovative and clever, but we gave up—laughing about it because I'd always forget to finish my speaking turn with "over."

27

LIFE MOVES ON

February 25, 2024

Jan's taken up stained glass as a hobby and has created some beautiful pieces for gifts. She made me an orange cat in honor of my beloved tabbies Frankie and Johnnie, a deer for her hunter son Ryan, a fox for her son Gregg's, new baby room, and a red cardinal for herself, in remembrance of Jon.

The moment he died, a red cardinal landed on her windowsill, inquisitively tilted his head and fixed on her, stayed for a while, and then flew off.

Periodically, since his death, Jan has noticed a cardinal visits her, particularly when she's struggling emotionally. She's hung a special feeder and water fountain to attract these birds. To keep them close. "When I nourish those birds, I feel connected to Jon," she said.

The family in Maine was invited to her condo for a pizza party today. Gregg, Jan's youngest son, was there with his wife Kate. He's outspoken and conversive now. As a child you could hardly get a word out of him. "Did you exchange grunts?" Jon dryly asked me, years ago when I mentioned I'd called him on his sixteenth birthday.

Ryan and his partner Janet were there as well as Joe and Ursula. Mom was not present. Everyone could relax and enjoy themselves.

The family is healing and life moves on. We are learning a new healthier way of being together without Jon.

At one point everyone was sitting around the table chatting and Jan looked out the slider and spotted one cardinal sitting in the lilac bush staring in at them and was convinced it was Jon visiting. I think it was too. Believing he still comes at family gatherings makes my heart swell with joy and pain, knowing how much he loved these get-togethers and how much everyone misses his energy and his humor.

Years ago, separated from her abusive husband, with two small children and no place to live, Jan moved back to the east coast from Seattle, and for one year, Jon generously took them in, until she could get settled, find a job and a place of their own. Nicole, her three-year-old daughter, struggled with separation anxiety whenever her Mom would leave the apartment, even to go down the street to the store. The upheaval and change were traumatic for her.

"Mommy, Mommy, Mommy!" she would cry, repeating incessantly, dewdrop tears streaming down her cheeks, as Jon tried to soothe her.

"She's coming right back Nicki; she's only going to the store. I'm here with you and you're okay. She won't be gone long." Reassuring her, pleading with her, repeating, "she's coming right back home. She just went to the store. She's not leaving you."

But it was useless. Nicki was inconsolable, hysterical, and nothing could distract her from her panicked state.

Jan, having been gone maybe a total of thirty minutes, came rushing up the back stairway to Nicki's anguished cries of "Mommy, Mommy!" and to Jon; standing in a corner, always the comedian in any dire situation, holding a sharp knife at his throat, simulating slicing his jugular.

Jon was close to my sister's children. Never wanting any of his own, he was nevertheless generous with his time and energy around them. A doting uncle. One year he drove my sister and Gregg and Nicki to New York City and they all stayed with us for Thanksgiving, sleeping upstairs in a friend's apartment in my building, since he was out of town. We took them around to see all the holiday sights and to the Macy's Thanksgiving Day parade. Standing eight rows deep in the crowd on the sidelines, Jon hoisted them up onto his shoulders one at a time, so they could catch a glimpse of the activities. He drove them down to New York City several times when they were young.

And he would converse with them like adults, never reprimanding but instead, reasoning with them, speaking openly and honestly.

"Don't let anyone see you picking your nose," he'd school Gregg. "It's not wrong. Everyone does it but just don't let them see you doing it. Do it in private, like in the bathroom and use the toilet paper to wipe your fingers."

It's March and although it still feels like winter, there are inklings of spring sprouting in Maine, an occasional blue sky and a sunny day. One single red cardinal appeared the other day at Jan's again, perched on a branch outside her window and sat there staring in at her as if probing for her attention.

That's odd, she thought but shrugged it off and went on with her day.

Later, looking at her phone, she noticed a missed message. It was Janet, her son Ryan's partner.

"Would you check in on Ryan to see if he's okay? I'm out of town and he called to tell me he was kayaking in the Nonesuch River, and a large tree branch broke off, landed on his kayak, tipped it over and knocked him into the freezing cold water. He had to swim to shore and hitch a ride back to his truck where he put in."

I'm sure Jon is looking down and watching out for his "little brother" Ryan. He's keeping an eye on us all.

Jan's stained-glass Jon cardinal

Early morning, March 2, 2024

I had a dream about Jon this morning. I was in a house with many family members and someone showed me an anthology book about South Portland, Maine with a young picture of Jon on the cover. I got excited and said, "Oh, I want a copy of that book. Does anyone know how I can get one?"

My deceased grandfather was present, and I wanted Bruno to meet him. He had passed away years ago and they had never met. Bruno and his daughter Daniela were somewhere else in the house, and I went in search of him.

Just then, Jon came walking down the stairs in a white track suit with black or navy-blue piping, spry and healthy and I was so happy to see him in this condition. I jumped up and ran over to hug him and tell him so. His body felt solid and strong in my embrace and his arm was completely healed but he was complaining, "I'm having wicked Gerd from this Prilosec."

I started schooling him, "You must eat raw ginger. Cut off

a little piece, chew it for as long as you can and then swallow. It's the instant cure for indigestion and reflux."

I awoke in the morning elated from the vivid dream and continued speaking to Jon aloud as if we'd been having a real conversation about the benefits of eating raw ginger. I realized I needed to heed my own advice, since I had been nauseous all night. I headed to the kitchen to cut myself a piece. "Thanks, Jon, for visiting and reminding me of that natural remedy. Say hi to Grandpa for me, will you?"

April 9, 2024

I joined a writer's circle last October and it inspired me to write about you Jon. I don't want to forget anything. Memories of us, growing up together, as adults, your illness, your dying, I want to remember it all. I'm afraid if I don't document it, my mind will get cloudy and the memories will fade.

It's been almost 19 months since you passed away. My grief has shifted and subsided and doesn't consume me. When it does surface, I allow for it and my mourning doesn't linger as long. The pain of loss still resides within the parentheses, but the time space gets narrower as I'm growing, changing and accepting life on life's terms. The windows between the parentheses grow wider and I'm healing and seeing clarity in my life by examining my truth. When you were sick, my first thought upon awakening every morning was about you. Now…not so much.

Grief is not only a feeling but a skill and I am learning it; evolving instead of revolving in my grief over you. I feel your spirit is further away now on a much higher plane, restored and complete.

You would say, "go live your life. Be happy, joyous and free." I want to do this for you. And at the same time, I want to honor and never forget you and everything you've been through. What we've been through together; all the good and the difficult times. Continuing to love you after death is my loyalty to you, my emotions that bubble up are my love that lives on.

So that's why I write. Sometimes, I wake in the middle of the night with a thought or a memory; get up and jot it down, so as not to forget. It's cathartic and I hope I'm honoring you but even if I'm writing this memoir for me, to immortalize you, that will be enough.

Mom is having a medium come to the house and asked me if I wanted to participate in a seance to see which spirits might come for a visit. I declined. I really don't want to disturb you or ask anything more of you, Jon. I want you to be free to rest in peace wherever you are. I wish Mom would leave you alone too. She's hoping you will visit her. Maybe send her second husband Bill down, in your place, instead.

A client is struggling with hand arthritis, and I will bring her some tools I've kept, to use in her next session. Your tools. As I opened the bag, a flood of memories came rushing back from our sessions over Facetime and all the hundreds of exercises we worked together in the hopes of gaining the loss of your mobility back, in my need to fix you. My guilt burdens me. I couldn't save you Jon. My mind wants to revert to feeling guilty rather than helpless, for it's a way for me to stay in control, and not relinquish the "what ifs?" "What if" we had tried some other alternative healing? "What if" there was a different treatment? "What if" we had caught the cancer sooner? "What if" we had helped you much earlier with emotional healing, maybe you wouldn't have developed brain cancer in the first place? My mind won't allow me to replace them yet with the "even ifs." "Even if" we had done all these things, it might still not have made any difference. I'm in the early stages of grief – it's less than two years since your passing.

It will be your 64th birthday at the end of this month, and I will be back in Maine visiting family around that time. I will feel your absence on a visceral level as I always do when I return to the area so I'll be on the lookout for any special signs from the birds just in case you want to say hello, but no pressure. I'm slowly learning to integrate the pain and the love. My heart is gradually shifting from the need to turn away from all the places that remind me of you, and instead, I'm cherishing the remembrances that resurface and honor you.

28

LOVELY DAY

Joey was six, Jan was eight and I was four years old. We were waiting upstairs in Joey's room for the call from the hospital. It was 1960 and fathers didn't participate in the birth like they do today, nor did we find out the sex of the unborn child back then. There were no MRI's or ultrasounds. Doctor Spock was the leading expert on what to expect when expecting. Birth, the most natural thing in the world, was left up to the medical "experts" to make all the decisions and parents obeyed orders.

Dad was home downstairs in the kitchen, baby-sitting us, busy cooking and doing chores, waiting close by the phone, so as not to miss the call from the hospital informing us when Mom would give birth. It was the only one we had; a green wall phone with a humongous, long cord. There was no answering machine back then, not that it mattered. Dad would be right there to pick it up on the first ring.

We kids were antsy and anxious, playing in the bedroom to pass the time. We wanted a baby brother badly, to evenly round out our foursome. On the bed in that room, we had stacks of thin children's Golden Books all piled up in neat little rows at the foot of the bed. About four rows, across the width. The stack must have measured six inches high. I don't know why we kept them there. Maybe easy access within reach for bedtime stories.

The phone rang and Dad answered it. We all shushed each other and held our breath. I remember him hanging up the phone and calling upstairs to us, "IT'S A BOY!"

We were ecstatic. Screaming and jumping up and down on the bed; thrilled to have a new baby brother! Two girls and now two boys! And all those books went flying off the bed.

Joey, Jon, Jan and Me, 1960

April 30th, 2024

Today would be your 64th birthday…gone at 62 years of age… so young to have left us. I believe you were "called" early, one of the special angels sent to us here on earth, for a short time for a reason. Maybe you had a mission, and it was completed? Or you gave up and went back to where all souls come from. You always said, you felt you wouldn't live a long life. I wonder how you knew?

Happy Birthday Gianni. I want to celebrate you instead of mourning your absence. I know you would want that too.

I dedicated my morning prayers exclusively to you…Walking to the subway, laughing…I must have been channeling you since the idea popped into my head to photobomb a couple of tourists taking a picture.

As I was tapping into a higher energy source—giving Reiki to a client, my phone chimes/timer went off by itself, at exactly 11:11, that bewitching moment when the veil is the thinnest between the spirit world and this world…hello Jon!

I left and walked through the park, breathing in spring, green grasses, observing all the colorful tulips for you while I listened to my 70's soundtrack. I looked down and there on the path in front of me was a little white feather next to a bigger bird feather…well hello Dad too! He's letting me know he's got you now and you guys are having a ball. What are you doing up there today to celebrate? I'm sure golfing, laughing and chowing down at an all-you-can-eat buffet. Don't forget the desserts.

I planned to go to Whole Foods, buy a birthday cake and flowers for you. While there, I took off my ear buds, noticing the piped in store music was one of your favorite BeeGees songs…"Ja…ja…ja…jiiiiiiive talking…You're telling me lies…"

I'm feeling your presence everywhere today Jon and I'm happy you are roaming free.

I walk by the baseball diamonds in the park and I think of when Bruno and I would play softball at the Brill estate in Bedford. We'd tell you about it and, being an athlete, you wanted so badly to play but never made the time to join us. How much you would have enjoyed it; knocking one out of the field. I imagine that you would come with us and everyone would be enchanted by your exuberant personality. The gals would flirt, be smitten with you, vie for your attention, and I'd be proud.

Never knowing who or which celebrity might show up at any given game, added excitement to the outing and we'd read about it on Page 6, the gossip column of the Daily News the following day. Michael Bolton came once and sang the national anthem.

"When I listen to Kenny G playing the sax it brings tears to my eyes," you confessed. You would have appreciated Michael Bolton singing acapella.

29

TOOTH WISDOM

March/April 2024

I have a toothache that won't go away. After exorbitantly expensive exploratory surgery (most likely covering the cost of my endodontist's ski vacation to Aspen), I'm still struggling sometimes with tooth pain, even after re-doing an old root canal and clearing out an infection underneath.

A program fellow told me at the time she was writing her memoir about a deceased parent, she too experienced problems with her teeth, and suggested I read *The Secret Lives of Teeth*, which delves into the metaphysical component to dental issues. I've been reading it with relaxed curiosity.

Peeka Trenkle, Homeopath/Herbalist, and all-around healer urges me to explore both—the physical as well as the metaphysical. What may start out as an emotional issue, if ignored, neglected and unprocessed, can become embedded in the physical body and expressed in symptomatic health issues. We can't heal what we don't feel and what we run from pursues us. The dis-ease needs to explode or else implode. Spiritual sickness might be considered the deepest level of unprocessed trauma and pain. (Evil is spiritual sickness manifesting in mass murderers such as with Hitler and Charles Manson.)

What has my brother's illness and death taught me about grief? I am a changed person. Jon and I had a special soul connection. My emotional enmeshment was extreme and distorted, paralleling his physical illness, and I was spiritually immature, unable to differentiate between empathy and compassion.

Am I more grief literate now? If, when I lose another close family member, will I go through the same grief process, or will it be different? I believe it will be different. I hope I'm able to lovingly detach and discern where I end and my loved one begins, whereas I was unable to do that with Jon. My emotional boundaries were blurred or non-existent. This grief experience has opened my mind and heart to a deeper understanding of death and dying. I'm learning there are many facets to the skill of grieving as I continue to walk with it.

30

DREAMTIME

June 5, 2024

I've been time traveling in my dreams and spending nights with Jon, with Lisa, with other family members, in many fantasy scenarios; with him living in New York City, going to parties together, renting an apartment here, (something he never did in real life, but I'd hoped he would). Exciting fun evenings together so when I wake up, I'm disappointed the night is over and I'm back here awake in my conscious world. Makes me curious and makes me question what reality is—our conscious or subconscious mind?

The Achuar, "dream people of the Amazon," build their entire lives on Dream Time insights and information. Each day before dawn, the community gathers in a ceremony to share and interpret their dreams. A remote tribe who had no contact with Western civilization until the 1970s, they ultimately sought help in saving the rainforest because of visions and answers they believed they received from deceased ancestors, during collective dream ceremonies.

Dreams can be a window into our soul's unmanifested desires. What we dream today can create our world tomorrow—what someone dreamt yesterday, we are living it today. So, should we give credence to what is revealed to us in Dream Time as a guidance to our conscious decisions as the Achuar clearly do?

I'm looking forward to time traveling with Jon tonight. Maybe it's all fantasy and wishful thinking but I'm going to revel in it a little longer and see what, if any, insights are revealed to me.

"Row row row your boat,
Gently down the stream.
Merrily, merrily, merrily, merrily
Life is but a dream."

The Eagle has landed (Jon's spirit).

3 1

EVOLUTION

August 11, 2024

We're in Maine this summer and for the first time, renting a place of our own in Freeport. It's far enough away from family, but close enough that we can visit easily. It's taken me this long to cut the cord. At 68 years of age, I feel like a grown up; staying on my own and not overly concerning myself with thoughts of whether I'm hurting people's feelings if we don't stay with them, especially my mother's.

I was afraid to tell her I wanted to do this! Can you believe it, Jon?

Of course he can. Fear of her backlash and then a guilt trip. But surprisingly she was fine with it. She's home now from a week in the hospital with congestive heart failure and with her aides coming and going, I think it's just too much for her to have house guests as well...Blessings!

The place that Bruno, my niece Nicki and I rented is lovely. Beautiful, serene, very private. I could kick myself for not doing this sooner, when Jon was alive. He would have loved it here.

Especially when he got sick and couldn't venture too far from home. This would have been an ideal spot for him to visit or stay with us…Regrets.

We hosted many visitors; family and friends, and cooked meals for everyone who came. It was fun, at first, but after several days of guests coming in dribs and drabs (rather than all on the same day, which we would have preferred), we were beginning to feel like sous chefs.

It was our third day in a row hosting, food shopping and cooking for guests when Nicki's siblings, (Ryan and Gregg) came for the day.

"Hey, do you guys want to go to the Harraseeket Lunch and Lobster for lunch today?" Nicki and I enthusiastically proposed in the hopes that we could get out of cooking, once again. "It's supposed to be a great place for local seafood."

Gregg and Ryan looked at us like we were crazy. "This is such a nice spot. Let's just hang here for the day."

Ok…We tried. One thing I can say is at a young age we all learned to cook and are adept at throwing together a meal at a moment's notice, everyone pitching in to help.

…My parents worked until 5 pm weekdays, so we siblings usually got the dinner cooked, ready and on the table, for when they both walked in the door at 5:30. One time we were baking potatoes and broiling pork chops and as I opened the broiler to check on them, the grease from the broiler pan had caught fire. Young Joey, not knowing that water and oil don't mix, threw a pan of water on the broiler in the hopes of extinguishing the fire, but it created the opposite effect. Flames shot up from the stove to the ceiling, and we screamed and, in a panic, evacuated the premises. We knew enough to get out of the house and save ourselves. Youngest Jon was sitting in the living room, obliviously watching cartoons and we grabbed him and hustled him out the front door.

We stood on the front porch terrified, anxiously awaiting our parents' arrival.

Oh Jesus! We're gonna catch holy hell! was the foremost thought occupying our young minds.

One of us, maybe Jan, since she was the oldest, creeped back inside to take a peek, and surprisingly, the fire was out, but, oh…my…God…the kitchen!! It was covered in black smoke and soot everywhere! The stove, the floor, all over the cabinets and countertops.

Like a scene out of "The Cat in the Hat," we quickly got busy, washing down and cleaning up everything, in the hopes that we could bring the kitchen back to normal before our parents arrived home and they wouldn't be any the wiser.

Success! Ok…Act natural. We were subdued and feigning nonchalance when they walked in. Everything was cleaned except for a large round black spot on the ceiling we missed, (smoke from the fire had shot up and left a tell-tale stain.)

My Mom looked up.

"What happened here?" she inquired with raised eyebrows.

Busted…We confessed our ordeal and learned how to put out a grease fire the hard way…

On another day in Freeport, Nicki's former grammar school friend Jessie and her two young boys were our guests for a day at the beach. Jan had brought a bevy of water toys. Blow up floaties, rafts, noodles, a paddle board, you name it—there was a wide selection to choose from to keep everyone entertained.

…Mom had bought us a blue and white Styrofoam 24-inch mini kick board at Woolworth's for a family outing at Pine Point beach. We were ecstatic over our new ocean toy, hardly containing ourselves, each taking a turn holding it, showing each other how we would use it to surf the waves.

Joey held it behind him eagerly, "I'm going to take it like this and put it on the water and sit on it!" enthusiastically demonstrating. CRACK!…The board broke into two twelve-inch pieces.

Shocked, devastated, we were horrified. Oh no! What happened? I was worried sick for Joey, ashamed of what we did, remorseful for my Mom and Dad, for the money they'd spent on this "extravagant" purchase; ($5.00 back in 1961 was considered splurging.) We tried gluing it together, but it wouldn't hold.

Nothing was said. I don't recall anyone being punished, or maybe I blocked it out. The lingering residual effect of the disappointment mirrored in my Mom's eyes was haunting enough. We tried to make the best of it at the beach with the two little broken pieces…

Everyone in Freeport was still asleep. I was sitting out on the deck, listening to the silence and the soft rustling of the wind tickling the leaves. As I watched the early morning sun flicker and filter through the trees, I could feel my aloneness constricting.

And I started crying thinking of Jon.

"I miss you Jon. It feels hollow and heavy at the same time here in Maine without you," I said aloud to no one.

Just then a bald eagle flew into my view and landed on an upper tree limb in front of me. He sat there twisting and turning his head as if to say *"I'm with you Joanne. I'm here with you."* He sat with me for ten minutes and then flew away, Jon's spirit appearing to me again, this time in a most magnificent way.

Are you alive in a different realm? Reincarnated? Our time on earth may be just a blip on the radar of our soul's existence. Maybe you've moved onto another level of consciousness or state of being. And do you have the capacity to travel now through different dimensions as an evolved spirit? Not in human form but perhaps as an eagle, a cardinal, an owl? Is this possible Jon…Feel free to visit me whenever you want.

32

SPRING LAKE

September 2024

We talked with Joe and Ursula about our favorite Jersey Shore area, Spring Lake, and if all things align—our schedules coordinate and the weather cooperates, we planned to spend three days and two nights with them at a bed and breakfast. After Labor Day the prices drop in half and September is the best time for the beach. The water is warm and the crowds have disappeared. I love squeezing out the last vestiges of summer for as long as I can.

We waited til the week before to book the rooms. Bruno was being considered for an acting job, a spot on an episodic and the shooting dates would conflict with our vacation plans. And wouldn't you know it; I got called for jury duty the last week in August. *When we make plans, the gods laugh.*

I was deep into practicing positive affirmations, visualizing my life and picturing it manifesting. The first day heading to jury duty, I repeated a mantra: "I will be released from jury duty with ease and go to the beach."

I got off the subway stop and looked up at the street sign to get my bearings. It was Beach Street—either a good omen or…be careful what you wish for…I quickly rephrased my mantra.

Yea! After three days of jury duty, I was released. The weather prediction for the following week was fabulous, and Bruno did not get the gig, so I immediately booked us rooms at the Spring Lake Inn, a lovely bed and breakfast three blocks from the shore.

Joe and Ursula had a long eight-hour drive from Maine, so we met them there around noon. After settling into our adjacent rooms, we convened on the front veranda, collected beach chairs and towels and headed to the ocean.

We delighted in showing Joe and Ursula around our favorite stomping grounds. Jan was supposed to come too but didn't, so we had this rare alone time with my brother and sister-in-law.

The weather was stunning—gorgeous beach day but rough surf. The only problem with September is dodging the effects of hurricane season, which creates fierce waves and undertows up and down the East Coast, so I'm cautious about entering the ocean without lifeguards on duty. It was after Labor Day, so we were on our own.

We all took a dip in the ocean, except Bruno. He refuses to enter the ocean unless we're in the Caribbean. I stayed in the water for a while, celebrating the last days of summer, floating on my back, riding the waves. Joe and Ursula took a quick dip—in and out. They're not used to the turbulence of these waters.

The dangerous surf entices me, and I must oblige otherwise I feel cheated, like I've wasted a good day at the beach, but I'm leery too. That same magnetic pull I felt as a child, scared and excited, butterflies in my stomach daring me to ride the Tilt-a-whirl and The Bullet at Old Orchard Beach amusement park. Ahh…my affinity with the sea.

Joe and I talked about the family, about my mother's care.

"I was a juvenile delinquent," Joe laughed. "I gave Mom so

much trouble. Taking care of her is the least I can do now to help her, after all I've put her through."

"No Joe, you weren't. It was your coping mechanism for an impossible situation at home with Mom and Dad. We all chose different survival skills to deal with the pain. Jan was mouthy, you acted out, I placated and Jon was obedient. We were doing the best we could under the circumstances. Don't blame yourself or take on caretaking duty for Mom because you feel guilty. It was never your fault nor your responsibility."

Ursula and I went for a walk on the beach and I confided in her.

"I'm worried about Joe having to take care of Mom as much as he does. I know how difficult she can be and it's a lot to put on him. Please let me know if it's ever too much and we'll brainstorm other solutions on how to get more help for her."

"Oh, I will," she said. "But you must know it's not too much for your brother. He loves doing what he does for your mother. Spending time with her. They have a great relationship. She treats him very differently than she treats you and Jan. And she's not going to live forever."

She spoke kindly of my mother though there is no love lost between the two of them.

"And know that Joe's just kidding when he says he was a juvenile delinquent. He doesn't mean anything. He's just playing."

"I don't believe that," I said. "Joe has always been sensitive and I'm glad he's opening up with us. I find when people say they're just kidding it's a way for them to deflect their truth."

"Maybe I don't want to know his truth," Ursula admitted.

We sat on the front porch at our bed & breakfast talking about Jon, and I showed Joe some videos that I had saved on my phone of Jon in those last days we all shared together at his house. Jon telling funny stories. We laughed watching them and I silently thanked Lisa for having the foresight to capture these moments for posterity.

We talked—relaxing and enjoying this time together without having to do anything. No pressure. When we were young, my mother struggled with just letting us be, always making sure we were occupied: working, cleaning, fixing, doing something.

Even now, when we go to Maine, Joe's usually manning the grill, or busy cooking, setting up and preparing everything at family functions. Without the busyness, there was space for us to engage on an intimate level, bonding us closer.

33
NEARING THE END

In July 2024, my Mom, at almost 94 years of age, was admitted to the hospital with congestive heart failure. My siblings asked for help, so I traveled to Maine and stayed eight days with her, spending nights alone at her condo and then back at her bedside in the hospital during the day. Wide-eyed and complacent, she appeared fragile and timid now, welcoming our support and all the attention and care she was receiving in the ICU.

In the mornings, we would scrutinize the hospital menu together, hoping for something new and delectable, and I would call in orders for her three daily meals. She was on a strict low sodium bland diet, so her options were monitored and extremely limited. Being a foodie, my Mom had tasted and evaluated pretty much all the main entrees, and the crusted chicken seemed to be the most palatable. We ordered it daily, with extra side sauces, and alternated between red and green Jello for dessert.

"What did you have for dinner last night?" my Mom would ask me when I arrived each day at the hospital. "Go ahead and cook up anything you find in the freezer at the house."

Jan was hosting a pickleball/cook-out the following Saturday at her place. She had already planned it before my mother got sick and we encouraged her not to cancel. I would stay with Mom, no problem. Party on without me.

I looked forward to spending quiet time alone with her. She looked frail and vulnerable like a scared young girl in her hospital bed. Humbled by her illness, her demeanor slipped into a docility that was much easier to manage and navigate.

We'd chat endlessly about the hospital food, what I had eaten for dinner, what Jan was planning on serving at the cookout, and the TV in her hospital room was set on the cooking channel, and it affirmed for me, Jon had inherited her obsession with food. They both loved talking about it.

"There're hotdogs in the freezer Jan. And Klondike bars." Take those for your cookout," she'd remind Jan everyday leading up to the party date.

At the end of her convalescence, she was improving and was being evaluated as to where she would transition; either a transitional rehab facility or directly home, depending on the physical therapists, nurses, and doctors' recommendations. We were pushing for the interim rehab facility so we could get her home set up, hire aides, and give her another week or two of full-time care, allowing for more confidence and strength building on her part, and more time for us to get everything in order.

She buzzed the nurse's aide for assistance to the bathroom.

"Do you need to use the pot?" asked nurse Cindy as she popped her head into the room.

"Yes," my Mom replied, patiently waiting while Cindy unhooked the oxygen tank and IVs my mother was attached to, but then Mom quickly stood up from the chair, on her own, and trudged to the bathroom wheeling her walker. She refused help and insisted on wiping and cleaning herself.

My mother, although emotionally needy and dependent, can be extremely determined, stoic and prideful. She prefers to do everything on her own, which gives the false impression that she's more capable and independent than she actually is. She'll rush through her exercises to prove a point. "See, I can still do things without help. I'm still strong and able."

"This doesn't look good for you to go to a rehab facility, Mom," I told her as I peeked at the nurses' chart attached to the door. The physical and occupational therapists had given her high marks on her exercise routines and recommended she be released to live independently at home.

"Don't pretend you're better than you are because it will work against you. I'm not saying fake your illness but just be truthful and ask for help if you need it."

My Mom should have been an actress. She got quiet and sat in reflection, (preparing for her close-up). When the nurse came back into the room my Mom slumped down in her chair and feigned weakness and whispered to her, "I overdid it this morning with the exercises. I pushed myself too hard and I'm exhausted now. Feel…feel my hands. They're cold."

"Actually, they feel pretty warm." the nurse cheerily replied, not falling for her act.

After a week's stay in the hospital, she was released directly home with an oxygen tank. We had been busy all week, setting up visiting nurse services, hiring extra aides, rearranging the condo for her safety, purchasing and setting up a hospital bed, in the small downstairs room, etc. There was much to do and learn.

Understanding and operating the oxygen tank, helping my Mom get used to walking around with a walker, while holding the long oxygen extension cord, winding it up or letting it out, depending on how far she was walking, and keeping it clear of the walker wheels was complicated and challenging. I let her get used to doing it by herself, but I watched her like a hawk and walked beside her, making sure she didn't trip and fall or roll over the cord with her walker. She was learning how to manipulate the excess cord and switch it from hand to hand like a cowboy in a rodeo, so that it wouldn't get tangled in the wheels. At one point, she stopped suddenly, and with a deadpan expression, simulated the sound effects, "shew shew shew," pretending to swing the extension cord like a jump rope (a Carol Burnett sense of humor flickering), releasing tension momentarily.

I stayed with her for three more nights at home so she and I could feel more comfortable, before I left. She needed someone with her at all times now. We still had a few holes to fill in her caregiver schedule.

I cooked delicious meals, my famous lemon chicken picatta, which she loved. "It's your signature recipe," she said. I had given her the recipe over the phone awhile back and she had tried to make it.

"I spent a lot of time massaging the lemon into the chicken. I thought you said to do that. It didn't come out the same as yours."

After dinner, she wasn't ready for bed yet, so we stayed in the kitchen together. She sat at the table with her legs elevated to prevent swelling, and I sat on the small white couch next to her. We pulled up a movie on Netflix, "The Girl on the Train," a murder mystery we had both seen before but wanted to watch again.

My mother has the annoying habit of asking questions during movies. It used to drive me crazy, and I'd get irritated and frustrated. But I was more patient with her now.

She'd ask a question and I'd hit the pause button on the remote. Like Siskel and Ebert, we'd discuss the situation, confer about it briefly, and then resume the movie.

I tried my best to ease her adjustment to all the challenges and changes to her health situation. She was tired, had been through a lot and so I kept things light. And knowing that Jan and Joe would be here to organize the rest of what was needed, once I was gone, gave her (and me) an enormous sense of relief.

I hardly slept that first night, in the downstairs bedroom, so I would be close to her in case she needed help. I would wake up every few hours, and tiptoe into her room to check and make sure the nasal cannulas hadn't fallen out of her nostrils. Checked the gauge to make sure she was getting enough oxygen.

I'd lean close over her sleeping body to see if she was still breathing and suddenly her eyes would pop open and she'd roll towards me out of a dead sleep and exuberantly announce, "Good morning! Let's have some coffee!"

She loved her coffee.

"Not yet, Mom, it's too early. Just go back to sleep," I said, relieved. "I was just checking on you to see if you were ok."

And she'd roll over on her side, away from me, and fall back to sleep like an innocent child.

A few more nights and I was completely spent from worry, anxiety and lack of rest but things were beginning to improve, so I was heading home to New York City. I had to leave at 5:40 a.m. to catch the early bus. I kissed and hugged my mother, wrenching with the thought of leaving her alone until the nurse would arrive at 8 am.

"I'll be fine by myself, don't worry." ...*How could I not?*

"The nurse is going to ring the front doorbell. Will you hear her?"

"Yes, and I'll just call out to her to come in. Leave the front door unlocked when you leave."

"Here's the questions for the nurse." I placed a pad of paper next to her bedside with a detailed list I had made. "Make sure you show her these," seriously doubting my Mom would be able to manage all this, write down or even comprehend the answers. She insisted she would be fine but in the Uber ride on the way to the bus station I didn't feel secure and called Jan. She agreed and drove over to be with Mom and advocate for her when the nurse came. *Thank you, Jan...*

34

FINDING BALANCE

The Fall Equinox, a time-honored moment in the year, when day and night are of equal length, represents balance and harmony in life. It's an opportunity for reflection. *Can I maintain a consistent connection between action oriented, earthly self, and my inner stillness of emotional and spiritual energy? Can I create harmony within the two worlds? What does balance look like for me?*

This September, we feverishly socialized with friends and family, attending outdoor concerts and shows, savoring every last drop of summer fun before resigning ourselves to "playtime is over," like children reluctantly returning to school.

Bruno left for Philly to visit Daniela for the weekend, and I relished my alone time and the chance to participate with gal pals in various events he didn't care to join—like a drumming circle, Sunday, in Marcus Garvey Park. Drumming speaks to my soul and I have a desire to learn.

The Indian summer weather was spectacular and I craved being outdoors. After Bruno left, I sped off on my bike down the west side Hudson River Park to Pier 17 Seaport on the East River.

I sat, drinking in the stunning views and soaking up the rays of the day, watching ferries and sailboats traversing up and down, feeling the cool breeze coming off the river and thought, *this is glorious. I gotta get out on a boat before the season ends.*

I texted my friend Delia, who is usually up for a last-minute adventure. She suggested we take the ferry ride out to Rockaway Beach the following day and have lunch at The Wharf, a cute low-key restaurant on the water.

Excited about our plan for tomorrow, I biked home. Feeling fatigued from the ride, I grabbed a slice of pizza and then laid down briefly before the scheduled massage I had booked for that evening, at the health club in my building. I felt decadent. Flying high in the extremes of fun, frivolity and self-indulgences.

The massage was intense and it was suggested that my back pain was directly related to kidney imbalances. According to Eastern philosophy the kidneys represent the nervous system and "might I need to drink more water?" Yes. Also, "might I need to address any stress or imbalances in my life?" Hmm…maybe.

Okay, food for thought but I was on a high now and mentally preparing for tomorrow's outing, researching everything I needed to know about the ferry, how to get there, how much it cost, what I should wear. Should I bring extra clothes because it might be chilly on the ferry ride home? Fifty questions squirreling around my mind and texting Delia back and forth for deets about what time to meet at Pier 11.

I got up early to get my usual weekly food shopping done at the farmer's market on the block, rushed back home, put everything away, watered the plants and packed a small bag for the trip.

The boat ride, Rockaway Beach—was magical. The Wharf, for lunch, right on the water. No tax and they only accept cash… okay…I didn't ask. I was having way too much fun. The most gorgeous sunset appeared as we passed Lady Liberty on our trip back.

I arrived home around 7:30 pm, totally exhilarated, yet fatigued, like a child saturated on sugar, unable to settle down and I was already ahead of myself, making plans for the next day.

I have a full slate of Sunday morning activities; my Super Soul Sunday, I call it. Beginning at 8:30 am—program meetings, remote work with my sponsee, a Kundalini yoga practice with follow-up group sharing, plus, this week, I added the drumming circle event I planned to attend with another friend, Lizzy.

I had a restless night, mental gymnastics that wouldn't dissipate but finally with the help of a Tylenol, I drifted off.

At 1:00 am I woke up to a crash somewhere in the apartment, bolted upright out of a dead sleep, and stealthily snuck out of bed, switched on the light and blurted, "Who's out there?" …Nothing…I checked the front door to make sure it was locked. And scanned the living room. No one and nothing seemed out of place.

"Humph?" I settled back down in bed with a relaxation tape and floated into dreamland.

I woke up physically and emotionally fatigued. Fearing I might be getting sick, which happens when I'm excessive. As I entered the bathroom, I noticed the squeegee that hangs in the shower had fallen completely off the wall into the tub, along with its container.

Was that you Jon? Trying to tell me something?

Michael Singer, in *The Untethered Soul*, writes about living in the Tao. The Tao refers to "the way of the universe," a middle ground—where our energies are balanced. He gives an example of a blind person who walks with a cane, tapping the cane from side to side, not to discover where to walk, but rather, to feel the edges, the extremes, where NOT to walk. I had been operating in the extremes all weekend and Jon was sending me a message—STOP, SLOW DOWN.

I stayed home that day, canceled the drumming circle, nurtured my soul with prayer and meditation, took a long nap, and cooked a healthy dinner.

Thank you, Jon, for the reminder.

In his four decades of research on near death experiences, Dr. Bruce Greyson hypothesizes *"if our minds can function even when our brains are offline, as the evidence suggests during NDEs, might it be possible that our minds could continue to function after our brains have stopped permanently—that is, after we die? Does consciousness continue?"*

Maybe our departed loved ones are still around, still with us, on a different plane of existence, a different level of consciousness.

Years ago, I visited Sedona, Arizona, a mystical place considered to be a spiritual vortex conducive to healing, meditation and deeper connection to the Divine. My tour guide friend Clay, suggested the possibility that Native American tribes inhabiting the area centuries before, had the ability to physically vanish when invaded by Spanish conquistadors. Yet their invisible spirits remain here.

Clay drove our group in his jeep through the red hills to his favorite sacred sites. We roamed around the pueblo ruins, and I felt connected to something beyond myself. A heaviness washed over me.

"Why does this place make me feel so sad?" I asked Clay.

"It could be that you're feeling your own grief," he suggested. The power of this area allows us access to our deeper emotional body. Buried feelings may arise to the surface to be healed."

I wonder if when we're at these sacred sites, can we sense a universal divine energy—the vital force that runs within us all? Do these vortexes act as an entry point or portal into the unconscious realm, so we can merge, feel and connect with the essence of everything? Dead or alive, we're swimming in the same water.

A short story by Ram Dass:

"There are two waves drifting along in the ocean, one a bit bigger than the other. The bigger wave suddenly becomes very sad and upset. The smaller wave asks what's wrong. "You don't want to know," the bigger wave says. "What is it?" the small wave asks. "No, really... it's too terrible. If you knew what I knew, you'd never be happy." The small wave persists. Finally, the big wave explains: "You can't see it, but I can see that, not too far from here, all of the waves are crashing on the shore. We are going to disappear." The small wave says, "I can make you happy with just six words, but you have to listen very carefully to them. "The big wave doesn't believe it—what does the small wave know that he doesn't—but he's desperate. After a while of doubting and mocking the small wave, the big wave finally gives in and asks the small wave to tell him. And so, the small wave says: "You're not a wave, you're water."

35

MOM'S TIME

Tuesday, September 24, 2024

"When am I going to see you again? Will you be coming back to Maine this year? You can stay with me; you can't sleep downstairs because I have my aides there but there's plenty of room upstairs. I'm getting my energy back. I've gotta hire the right girls. I'm so confused. I can't keep it straight who's coming when, and this is Deb's last week before she goes to Florida and I'm nervous about her leaving me," my Mom rambled on over the phone.

My first inclination was to say *"No, I'm not coming back this year,"* but I stopped myself short.

"Sure Mom. I'll come up sometime at the end of next month. Just me alone and spend time with you. But you do have a replacement for Deb, right? Someone is there with you?" I needed reassurance.

"Oh yes," she said. "A new girl is coming shortly, but we still need to hire a few more to cover time slots that haven't been filled. It's so much work for your poor brother Joe.

He's so good and he's doing it all. It's a shame Jan won't help us. We need her! Can't you ask your sister to help out? Geez it's all in Joey's lap and it's overwhelming for him. Could you call her and ask her?"

"I did Mom, but she said no." My sister had detached with an ax a month ago from my mother for her own sanity, health and peace of mind. The two of them are like oil and water and had another major falling out.

"Did she say why?"

"No, just that she can't, Mom." I couldn't/didn't want to open that can of worms.

"I don't understand her! Why is she like this?"

"I don't know, Mom." Again, playing dumb.

"If you were here, I know you'd help out, wouldn't you?"

"Yes," I reassured her and left it at that.

She chatted a little longer wanting to make sure she had sent Bruno a birthday card back in July. She had. She was diligent about remembering birthdays and anniversaries and made a point to acknowledge them with cards.

"I'm dying. I feel the end is near. I'm old and I want to go." She'd been dramatically saying that for years. But this was different. I believed her this time.

"I want you to have my wedding ring. And the necklace Jon gave me. Will you wear them? After I die, you can have them."

My Mom exuded an anxious agenda on our phone calls over the past few weeks. She seemed to be checking off lists. Completing things. And then she'd abruptly end our conversation and hurriedly get off the phone. Things were changing.

Two days later, I got a text from my sister. "Ann says Mom's still sleeping and it's 2:30. She has to leave before the relief aide comes and is asking me if I could come over to sit with Mom until she does."

"Did she check if she was breathing?" *Duh*, I thought to myself. Lights on but nobody's home sometimes with Ann. But my Mom loved her like a daughter. She would give her unsolicited advice, could boss her around but Ann retaliated; called my mother "your Highness" to her face, and got away with it! Those two were like an old married couple.

I was irritated with my sister. My Mom had always been harsh with her, and I understood her need to pull away but still… right now? At this crucial juncture? Couldn't she tolerate the abuse a little longer? Mom wouldn't live forever.

"Maybe she's just tired. She sleeps a lot these days. Maybe she's just overtired today," I repeated.

My sister couldn't go because she had her art class. The visiting nurse was coming anyway. So, Jan called Joe, who lives farther away and he drove to my mother's place to check on her condition.

A few hours later, something didn't feel right. I called my mother's house and Joe answered.

"I'm with the nurse now and she believes Mom's had an incident." (code word for stroke). "She's unconscious now," his voice quaked.

"Should I come up?"

"Yes. We're not sure how much time she has left."

"I just spoke with her two days ago! She seemed fine then." I was incredulous.

I made arrangements for Bruno and me to take the Concord Coach Plus Bus up to Portland the next day. But death arrogantly skulked in through the back door. My mother passed away that night before we arrived.

She just couldn't wait for me, I thought to myself. Typical of my mother. She was determined, stubborn and when she wanted to do something, she had to—immediately, on her terms. She wanted to go and nothing (like me not being present to help her cross over), was going to stop her from leaving.

I felt gypped. Again. I wanted to be there to help Jon transition. Not allowed. And now my Mom. Too much of a hurry, she couldn't wait for me to help her. Who am I kidding? At this stage, she didn't need me anyway.

Upon hearing my mother had passed, I felt adrift, untethered, like a helium balloon floating erratically in the sky. I had been having stomach pains and bloating discomfort the past few days, my body reacting, unable to digest this new information. My brother and sister were experiencing the same physical sensations. Our last thread of connection to "Mother;" the energetic umbilical cord had been severed.

We met with the funeral director, Alisa, the following day. She was empathetic and congenial. Considerate. Professional. My brother, sister and I were nervous and gentle with each other, but also reactive and edgy since we each had unique relationships with my mother and our feelings were conflicted and unprocessed.

Joe and Jan had been at my mother's bedside after she passed, waiting for the undertaker. She had wanted to keep wearing her wedding bands, a special gold necklace of talismans for Jon and a bracelet. But she instructed they be removed upon her death and be given to Jan and me.

"This really doesn't feel right," Jan cried as she struggled with my mother's contorted body to remove the bracelet from her wrist. "It's macabre. I feel sick doing this."

"Just do it," Joe snapped. His emotional bandwidth stretched beyond its limit. He had closed my mother's eyes but her mouth gaped in a frozen grimace, and he struggled to get the rings off her fingers, compelled to honor my mother's last wishes.

As was expected, my Mom had planned, bought and paid for the entirety of her funeral and the arrangements, and Alisa shared her wishes with us but we still had decisions to make. Dying is expensive and complicated. It took several hours to go over everything and once finished, she asked if one of us would like to identify the body, lying in state before cremation.

"I would," I spouted, hoping that seeing her would give me some sense of closure. Joe and Jan chimed in as well.

"She'll be in the next room, off to the right lying in the coffin," Alisa gently prepared us. "She's dressed in the nightgown she wanted to be cremated in and we've covered her in a sheet pulled up to her chest. Her hands are folded with her rosary beads, and the picture of her sons is with her, which she wanted. Her eyes are closed and her mouth is shut so she looks peaceful."

Ouch…She didn't want to take a picture of Jan and me with her too? Italian mothers and their love affair with their sons—they can do no wrong. Bruno told me his mother once said, "You can always get another wife, but you can't replace your mother." Daughters (and wives) get thrown under the bus.

My mother was difficult and challenging, but I forgave her completely.

I went to her lying in the casket.

"Hi Mom," I leaned over her, touched her face, her hair, kissed her forehead, gently pressed my hands on her shoulders and her heart while a cascade of tears and grief and love poured out of me.

"Why didn't you wait for me to come? I wanted to help you and hold your hand until Jon and Dad could welcome you to the other side," I murmured as I laid my hands upon her body transmitting Reiki; love energy, through me to her, for her, for me… for healing. I heard Joe mumbling through tears and felt his hand gently stroking my back.

We all spent time there with her in reverence, touching, feeling her, with our hearts aching, standing in our grief.

Joe was the closest to my mother. His grief was transparent. Jan was subdued. She had been estranged from Mom so I can only imagine what she felt. A mixture of sadness, guilt, anger and fear? She was restrained at the casket. Never touched her. Maybe she didn't feel the need to or was afraid to? Instead, she spoke clinically.

"It looks like the blood settled on that side of her face. That's where she had the stroke." But that's my sister's way. Practical. There was a persistent challenge in their relationship.

Once we were in the parking lot she confessed, "I'm glad I saw her lying peacefully at rest, to replace that horrible last image I had of her in my mind."

Bruno and I stayed at my Mom's place. I sought and nestled within her things.

"Hi Mom," I said when we got back to the condo and I laid down and curled up on her empty hospital bed. I talked to her as if she were still there.

"Mom, it was good to see you today. You looked at peace. Are you? I wish you had waited for me to get here but I know you're with Jon and Dad and that's all that really matters. I miss you, Mom. I love you."

I felt her spirit and her energy in the house. We turned on the TV Christian Mass for her, so used to her blaring it at full volume, but I found it comforting today. Sitting around, looking through her things, I tried on her sequined jacket that hung in the closet (like I used to do when I was a kid), and I wore it while reading through drawers full of cards; Mother's Day, birthdays, Christmas, Easter, anniversaries, Valentine's Day and get-well cards; she saved every last one of them. (Jon had done that too. Lisa said he kept every single card that was ever given to him.) I took my time. I was in no rush to clear out her things and clean up her place.

And just then, I realized I had been "with her" to help her cross over. When Joe told me over the phone the end was near, I hung up, quickly made arrangements to get up to Maine and then went to my "altar," which I have set up in the bedroom of our apartment, lit candles and spent time sending her distance Reiki healing to comfort her and guide her spirit. When I finished sending it, I got the call that she had passed away.

Whenever Bruno and I would come to Maine for a visit and stay with my Mom at her condo, we'd get up to catch the 6:30 am bus back to New York City and she'd always get up too, have coffee with us and insist on packing us a lunch of sandwiches, fruit, chips, and whatever was left over from our stay together, as if we'd never eat again. (By the way, that is something my grandparents always did. We never left their house without a bag full of groceries to take home).

I'm not much of an early morning talker, but Mom would annoyingly be chatting up a storm and then insist on standing at the front door with the light on, waving goodbye to us as our Uber car drove away.

It was different this time. So, we left the condo to catch the bus, leaving an empty quiet house, no morning chit chat or frantic lunch packing, no light above the front door and I had no need to look back because she wasn't there waving goodbye to us.

Oh… how you don't miss certain things until they're gone.

I went back to Maine two weeks later for the Funeral Mass my mother had pre-orchestrated in complete detail down to the flower arrangement she wanted—white flowers with six red roses interspersed, representing each immediate family member.

"Can you send me some pictures of me that I could use for my obituary?" she'd asked me months earlier. I selected several; a few recent ones that I loved, and also ones from her younger years, and, of course, she picked a glamorous, much younger photo. It always cracked me up when my parents would comment while watching TV celebrities, "boy he's gotten old," as if time stood still for them.

Bruno couldn't come with me this time because ironically, he booked a television episodic and had to be on set in New York City for filming the day of the service. We agreed he should stay and do the job, since he'd said his goodbyes to my Mom two weeks earlier.

I would often tell my mother about Bruno's numerous auditions.

"Is he ever going to get one of these jobs?" she would bluntly ask. "It seems like an awful lot of work for nothing. I hope it's worth it."

I think she'd be pleased he did book this one. Or maybe not. It prevented him from attending her swan song.

We met at the condo, the morning of the service, bright and early. I had stayed there overnight by myself and found it consoling. Joe, Ursula and Jan arrived early so we could gather ourselves, sit and cry together, before the limousine my mother had ordered showed up to drive us to the church. I had written a eulogy which I would read, Joe would carry the "gifts" to the altar. Ryan and Nicki, would each do a reading from the bible. It was a private service so there were very few people in attendance, mostly family, some extended, and a few friends.

… "I want my ashes spread over the ninth hole at Riverside golf course to be with your brother and father," my mother had requested.

"But why Mom?" I was surprised. "You always hated golf. And what about Joe, Jan and me? We don't even like golf. And what about Bill?" It made no sense to me but my Mom had her private reasons…

The funeral priest spoke with a Jamaican Creole accent, and it was difficult to understand him. I chuckled remembering my mother always pointing out "my Black friend" in the audience of the Catholic mass she watched daily on TV. I guess he wanted to witness her send off.

Afterwards, we returned to the condo for a celebration, a gathering with friends and family. We served sandwiches, desserts, wine and beer. I felt fragile and dissociated, deluged with everyone's expressions of grief. People sometimes say the most inappropriate things.

"Are you going to rent the condo?" a concerned neighbor asked.

"I'm not sure yet," I lied, knowing very well we weren't.

"Because if you want the name of an agency that advertises to medical personnel for short term housing, I can get that for you. My friend does that and the prospects are all highly reputable and vetted."

"What are you going to do with your Mom's car?" Suzie inquired. "I'd be interested in buying it from you."

Is now the time for these discussions? She's barely cold? I screamed inside, as I wearily listened to them, forcing myself to stay present and non-reactive.

Many guests shared their litanies of illnesses or stories of their own family deaths; a natural need to identify. I nodded in agreement and feigned sympathy. It was draining and exhausting.

I had a few more days alone in the house before heading back to New York City and I welcomed the alone time. My mother's death triggered my dormant grief over Jon. It was fresh and raw again.

I cleaned up the house and started going through closets and found a box of baby shoes, recognizing a pair of Jon's. He wore orthopedic hard soled shoes as a child. They were supposed to correct flat feet. They didn't. I gently lifted them out of the box, pressed them close to my chest, tears falling…remembering how we teased and made fun of his "clodhoppers." He would get angry and upset and kick us.

I'm sorry Jon.

I brought them back home to New York and have them in my bedroom under a framed picture of him as a young boy, sitting in his suspendered shorts, short sleeve Peter Pan collared shirt and knee socks, one leg tucked underneath the other, strategically posed by the photographer, smiling sweetly at the camera, wearing those shoes.

Occasionally, I like to pick them up when I walk by, cradle them in my hands. I touch the weathered soles, run my fingers over the smooth white tops and slightly blackened rounded toes, worn at the edges—evoking warm memories of my little brother.

36

SAFE ARRIVAL & STAYING CONNECTED

Communications persist from the beyond. It's out of season, but Gianni's plant bloomed again, letting me know Mom arrived safely, peacefully joining Dad and him, and that all has been reconciled and forgiven.

October 15th is my wedding anniversary. Mom was adamant about sending cards and made sure she sent one to us before she left, for our anniversary and one for my birthday, October 29th.

Bruno and I celebrated 22 years together with an early dinner at Eataly, walked home in the sunshine and settled in to watch a Ben Kingsley movie, "An Ordinary Man."

As we watched his performance, suddenly, the volume indicator on the TV screen scrolled up to maximum level, as if one of us had accidentally sat on the remote. We looked around and the remote was nowhere near either of us.

Hi Mom. I know you would have enjoyed this film.

It's November 2nd, All Souls' Day, a Christian observance for remembering the departed and a time to connect with spirit guides.

While lying on the couch, listening to a meditation app on my phone, I dozed off into an anxious dream—I couldn't get the

Funeral Mass organized and woke up to the crickets chirping on my phone, alerting me to a text message.

Relieved it was only a dream and the funeral was over, I picked up my phone to read, noticed it was open to a picture of Jon's obituary page, I had previously saved in photos, and the text message was from my friend Lizzy.

I shared his obit with Lizzy and re-read it myself, digressed into ruminating about his widow, Lisa, and google searched her, sleuthing for any new information. Ok…I've done this before. I wonder how she is doing? Should I call her now that Mom is gone? To see how she is? Try and reconnect with her?

As I was surfing the net, PING! My mother's memorial page popped open on my phone, with her full face staring up at me. The ping indicated a new memory had just been posted to her page, and at the same time, the smoke alarm battery began beeping in the apartment.

"Jon, what does this all mean?" I asked aloud. *"Are you trying to tell me something? Should I reach out to contact Lisa?"* The beeping continued until I pulled the ladder out of the closet, climbed up and unplugged the alarm.

I waited for a clear sign. Any sign. Nothing. Just then, Bruno walked in the door. I told him what had occurred and asked for his input.

"NO!" He said. "Don't you get it? It was a clear warning sign from Jon to leave Lisa alone, let her be and focus on living YOUR life!"

My phone rang the other night during dinner. My Mom always called at that time. *It's Mom,* I thought. Then caught myself and realized, *no…she's gone.* It's strange…there's more free time and room in my life now. I'm resettling into the newness and adjusting to this space.

37
CHRISTMAS 2024 & THE CONDO

My brother Joe, my sister Jan and I have inherited my mother's condo in South Portland. She was very specific about how we are to use it.

Nicki needs a place to live for six weeks while she's in Maine and I inquired, "Might she be able to stay there? After all, she's family. Could we bend Mom's directives a bit? No one is occupying it now."

Joe, as the Trustee, says no. He believes we are obligated by law to follow the instructions to the letter, and to respect and honor my mother's wishes. Jan and I would like to be more flexible, and broader in our interpretation of the Trust but Joe thinks it would be illegal and disloyal to Mom.

Jan is furious. I was too, at first. *I can't believe we are legally bound to follow what the Trust dictates? We need clarity!*

But only time will reveal more and hopefully things will change. It's all so new and we're in the early stages of grief. Everyone is adjusting.

There has been a luxurious opening created for me in my life with this inheritance. When I was young, my prayers included praying for a place where the whole family could come and gather, friends and family to celebrate holidays and vacations together. I often dreamed of owning such a place that required low maintenance on my part. And in the past twenty years I've been fortunate to have generous clients who have allowed me the use of their country homes. Now, my mother granted us this gift, a place of our own.

Optional Yankee Gift Swap at 3pm!!
REDUCE REUSE RECYCLE! (instead of gag gift)
Bring something you've received as a gift in the past, OR something you have at home that you just don't want anymore. Clean it up, wrap it and regift it, anonymously! It can be anything- That's what makes it fun! One person's trash is another person's treasure! Let the swapping begin!

This Christmas, Bruno and I will be staying for two weeks in Maine at the condo. Our condo. We're opening the place for family and friends to join us, for a celebratory gathering, and are considering making it a yearly tradition. We plan to escape the city heat and spend the month of August next year, in Maine, at the condo as well. Explore how that feels for us.

Thanks Mom.

I love New York City but having a place I can get away to is a welcomed luxury. Just knowing we have it, softens my thoughts and expands my heart. I feel more available, more tolerant of others, and more at ease. I think it will help Bruno too, since he's craving additional living space and room to breathe without the onslaught of crowds that we deal with daily in the City.

It's getting closer to the date for us to leave for the holidays and old childhood anxieties about Christmas with family are re-surfacing. The dynamics between my sister, my brother and I have changed since my mother's death. Or maybe now that the referee is gone, we've let down our guard and are more capable of being honest with ourselves and each other.

There's an old fear, like a knee jerk reaction and I am young; 10 years old, still nervous, hoping everyone will get along, and I unconsciously and automatically assume my former family role of peacekeeper. But I'm bringing with me all the tools I'm learning in my ACA recovery program. How can I respect myself and yet be there for others in my family? Do I have to sacrifice my truth to maintain the status quo? I don't want to and yet there's sadness around letting go of my position in the family unit. How do I operate now? I don't know how to do this.

There's a fair amount of discomfort, for a time, when re-leasing old patterns of behavior even when we know they're not healthy and don't serve us anymore. *"Change back!"* a frightened voice inside me shouts.

A fellow traveler with years of recovery under his belt, shared his experience meeting with an old buddy for lunch. His friend snidely commented, "Oooh Bob, you're on time for a change."

"I think you're referring to the former version of myself." Bob replied.

It's confusing because I miss my old self. She feels familiar and comfortable. You'd think one would naturally gravitate towards emotional sobriety, but it makes sense that it's unattainable without consistent effort. The voyage is not easy.

Accepting this truth allows me compassion for myself in transitioning and helps me stay the course when I feel the urge to backtrack to old behavior and my former role in the family unit.

Humans are creatures of routine. Do you gravitate to the same seat in a classroom? I do. Melody Beattie, renowned author of numerous self-help books says, "it takes repeating something twenty-one times before we create a new habit."

The brain acts like a superhighway of neural pathways; developed over time, from unconscious thoughts based on learned behaviors from parental role models who didn't necessarily make the healthiest decisions themselves. Adhering to different modes of thinking and behaving that follow our own truths, instead of ones we've adopted, passed down to us from others, is like carving out new dirt roadways in the brain. I've been on this super strata for 69 years and have become accustomed to the route. The change, shift and recovery take time.

I'm in the hallway now. Not where I used to be and not quite where I want to go, but the only way to get there is to endure a time of difficulty and awkwardness, feeling uncomfortable in my skin, trying out new behaviors, because I trust, eventually this practice will lead me to the change I seek in my life.

The bus ride up to Maine for our Christmas vacation was long, but as passengers, we could sit back and relax. I've been struggling with a chronic urinary tract infection that won't heal. Or

I could be passing a kidney stone, my internist suggested. Not fun. Coincidentally my Mom was a quarry, making stones and struggling with chronic UTIs, all her life. My homage to you, Mom.

I've packed my pharmacy of meds, supplements, teas, and tinctures to take and, worst case scenario, I can always get help if need be. I know where to go, in the area, to receive emergency medical attention.

It's cold and the bus arrives in Maine late at night. It smells like snow. Jan picks us up.

"Look!" I point to the sky, thankfully settling into the heated front passenger seat of her car. I notice the monstrous full moon hanging low in the sky. It's unique and bright. Eerily comforting.

"Wait til you see the condo! It's all decorated and looks cozy and inviting," Jan says. "Nicki and I bought a real Christmas tree, loaded it on top of the car ourselves and set it up in the living room. I cleared out the kitchen and threw out a bunch of shit, rearranged furniture and things. I'm not so sure Joe likes it but I think you'll like the improvements I've made to the place. The kitchen cabinets are so dark and dated."

She texted me on the bus, "Do you want me to pick you up Thai food for dinner?" *Thoughtful…*

"Yes thanks!" I texted back. We were starving. As we sat down to eat at my Mom's kitchen table, now *our* kitchen table, Jan went through a litany of what she had done to fix and clear out the place, itemizing where things were now located, in which drawers and what shelves, and what else needs to be done to "update this old place."

"It looks beautiful, Jan." I think it's lovely just the way it is. "Thanks Mom," I say aloud. I'm elated. It really is a gift.

Jan has a flair for decorating, something we all inherited from my Mom. She had decorated the tree, strewn evergreens and candles artistically over the mantelpiece, placed candles in every window, hung wreaths with handmade Norman Rockwell red bows on the front and back doors, and set festive decorative lights by the front path, creating a warm and inviting atmosphere for us and for our guests for the Christmas party.

…It was the 1960's and the Maine Mall Shopping Center had yet to be built so downtown Portland was the only place to shop. Taking the bus at night into Portland for Christmas shopping on Congress Street was magical. The area was decked out in festive attire with green garlands and multi-colored lights draped every twenty feet above the street, creating inviting swag archways of glistening Yuletide. Tinkling of bells could be heard from the Salvation Army volunteers who stood huddled in their long black coats and caps, demurely signaling for donations from the onslaught of pedestrians passing by.

In our boots, winter coats and fake fur bunny hats, we'd trudge through the snow-covered sidewalks and roam from store to store with all the other evening shoppers. Porteous, Rines Brothers, Grants, Benoit's and Woolworths were the only department stores in town. We'd make an extra stop at a tiny store on the corner of Congress and Middle Street, to purchase a special treat—the mint chocolate bar from Fanny Farmer's candy store. As soon as I'd open the door to that small store, a waft of chocolate would engulf me, and my mouth would begin to salivate in anticipation of that tasty delight. What a dream job it would be to work there! All the chocolate your heart desired. Maybe that's why I only saw older women behind the counter. Teenagers would have bankrupted the place.

After finishing the shopping we'd stand and wait for the bus, our breath—puffs of smoke in the raw night air. Shivering in the cold with toes turning numb, we'd shift from one foot to the other and stomp our feet to stay warm. The bus stop was across the street from our favorite and largest department store—Porteous Mitchell and Braun. Gazing up above the store awning at the row of resplendent decorated Christmas trees, we'd wait for the return bus home in awe…in reverence. The hope of Christmas—it felt like anything was possible…

"We'd better go shopping for the party early tomorrow morning because it will be a mob scene at Costco," Jan complained.

I'm back in my kid sister role where she knows best so I allow her to take the lead.

The next few days we prepared for the party. The invite said *"potluck party, bring something to share,"* but we shopped in excess just in case no one read the fine print.

We bought a plethora of frozen finger foods; chicken tacos, shrimp, chicken skewers, baby quiches and spanakopitas, (span-iko-pee-pee as Jon would say in his toilet humor), meatballs and crab balls, crab dips and hummus, crackers, chips, cheeses, cookies and desserts. Plus, wine, beer and prosecco. More than enough. But we can't help ourselves. Fear of running out of food at a party is in our DNA.

New York City friends—Bill, Val and their 14-year-old son Wilder—were arriving the night before the party and would be our guests staying at the condo for three nights. A welcome buffer for family dynamics.

The party was a success. Lots of people arrived in festive moods and ugly Christmas sweaters and everyone brought food and drink. I spent most of the time refilling and rearranging food platters—an excuse to avoid others and isolate myself in a room full of people.

…I was 13 and my mother hosted a bridal shower for my cousin Judy. Our house was filled with women's vibrant energies and loud voices; aunts, cousins, friends, sitting in a large circle in the living room, chatting and laughing, oohing and ahhing over the gifts Judy opened and passed around for everyone to examine. At one point I looked around and didn't see my Mom.

I went in search of her and found her in the kitchen sitting by herself, on the step stool, in the corner, hunched over and curled up in a ball, her feet tucked up under herself on the high step.

"Are you okay Mom? What are you doing in here?" I was concerned.

"Hiding out," she confessed sheepishly…

At the time I didn't understand. I do now…

The Yankee Gift Swap concept of reduce, reuse and recycle was a hit, and everyone joined in the fun and excitement. Jon would have CHERISHED the game. He was an extreme anti-consumerist.

"Don't throw that out! I can reuse it," alarmed when I would attempt to trash his one single sheet of paper towel, folded in half, which he used as a napkin, if it wasn't soiled.

It's the third Christmas without Jon on earth and it's still hard for me. I miss him. In the midst of the festivities his absence was palpable. My Mom was the needle, but Jon was the thread. His spirit was the gravitational pull that kept us sewn together.

Both forces are gone now. What's left in their place, is an emptiness, once filled with family traumas that kept us connected. We've been conditioned to deal with crises. My mother trained us well. And we've bonded through the on-going family strife— Dad's illness and his living situation, Jon's illness and subsequent early death and always…my mother. These struggles have been eliminated. The concerns and problems that kept us connected have evaporated.

It feels uncomfortable together without crises to focus on. Unusual. Foreign. And we're left to sift through our shared memories of the past. A wise woman once said to me, "the purpose of family is to get together to reminisce about old times."

Oh, why couldn't you have outlived Mom so we could enjoy this time together at the condo? I regretted Jon's death throughout the week. *What would it be like to connect without her oppressive energy*

It was time for the Yankee Swap. Gifts were spread under
the Christmas tree in the living room and we drew numbers out
of a hat. Number one went first and opened a gift. Number two
picked a gift, opened it, and then either kept their gift, or traded it
for number one's gift. And on it went.

Joe, Ursula and I leaned in the doorway between the kitchen
and the living room, chatting about each opened gift and the camaraderie of the swapping. It was the first time I connected with
Joe since my mother's funeral, and I felt close to him. Our hearts
were lighter now.

I made a mental note to myself to call them more often, find
a way to stay in contact, include Ursula more in conversation so I
don't lose my brother Joe.

Ten-year-old Lucy, dressed in Brooklynese hipster fash-
ion with a red ribbon artistically draped around her head and
an off the shoulder white sweater, took the swap seriously. She
had searched her house to find the right gift to bring, wrapped it
herself, and as the time approached for the game to begin, grabbed
her little sister's hand and said, "let's head into the living room
now so we can get a good seat up front."

There's always one gift in this game that is everyone's favorite
and gets swapped around the room. This year it was a crystal salt
lamp that Deb brought, and lucky Lucy was the final recipient.

Big board game players, Bill, Val and Wilder spent countless
hours with us over the next few days, playing Monopoly, Scat-
tergories and Dominoes. We cooked, went bowling, and Wilder,
a rambunctious 14-year-old, wanted to skate outdoors and was
relentless—hounding his parents to take him. It was freezing out.
I suggested a few ponds they could try in the area. Always the
doting Dad, Bill took Wilder out one frigid night.

…My Dad was athletic, a speed skater and could skate backwards like a pro. He would take us skating at Clark's Pond in South Portland while my Mom sat huddled in the car holding the thermos of hot chocolate for us to warm up with, once we got cold and had enough.

"Stand right here and look off at the trees," my Dad instructed me. And my six-year-old self, scared but trusting, obediently stared straight ahead, as I stood in the center of the pond, wobbly on my little white double runners. Then WHOOSH! Out of nowhere, to my surprise, my Dad in his slick black skates, swooped in behind me, scooped me up in his arms and sashayed us fast fast fast around the pond. It was thrilling!...

I loved having Bill, Val and Wilder as our guests over Christmas, yet at times, it felt too much. Maybe it was too soon. Maybe, I needed more time to grieve and adjust to the newness of everything. They're like family. I love my family, but I need space from them too…

Jon would often share with me his mixed emotions over being married to Lisa yet living apart. I could sense he wanted more time together with her, but he also cherished his alone time. He would stay at his camp in northern Maine for days alone, on silent retreat, without a soul around for miles.

He wrestled with his heart. "How could it be possible to have these opposing feelings at the same time?" It was unsettling and didn't make sense to him. I was conflicted and struggled with my own yin/yang. We wanted clarity, resolution—black and white answers.

"I can spend days upstate not speaking to anyone and feel absolute peace. Lisa and I are better separate," he'd reason it out.

"But you're a very social person too, Jon. You need both," I tried to convince him, and justify my own vacillating feelings.

Today, instead of thinking it must be either or, I'm learning integration—accepting how it's possible to hold space for two opposing feelings at the same time. I wish I had understood and embodied emotional complexity when Jon was alive. Maybe I could have helped him understand it and accept it too.

38

COMPARING GRIEFS

Grief washes over me in different colors. Since my Mom's death rekindled my Jon grief, it was difficult not to compare the two. The loss of my Mom, at age 94, emerges in soft pastels, Easter pale pinks, fuchsia, yellow. It's gentle. Maybe it's because my mother lived a full life. Losing my brother to brain cancer, at 62, envelops me in dark vibrant blue, vivid green, red, sometimes black.

I knew exactly what my mother wanted for her ending. She spoke about death and dying often.

"Oh, don't talk like that," I'd dismiss her. It was off putting at first; melodramatic, and I would change the subject, denying my own fear of death.

But later, I would engage with her in these discussions.

"I wonder if this is hell on earth?" She'd reflect. "There's so much strife and pain here."

We were open with each other; curious about death, dying and the afterlife. My mother wanted to die in her last years. She was ready to go and would convey to me in detail her death arrangements. I would listen. This helped her feel complete and somewhat settled at the end of her life and it had that effect on me as well.

After the initial untethered period following her death, I've settled into an acceptance of her being gone, and in my heart, I truly believe she is at peace now, maybe with Jon, with Dad. I have resolution with her.

Four years of anticipatory grief, throughout my brother's terminal illness, his subsequent death and his choices for end of life, have taken me much longer to reconcile and process than my mother's passing, and I battle with the complexity of it all.

Jon left us too early and I was barred from witnessing his ending. I still question the veracity of his heart's dying wishes, what was conveyed to us through Lisa. Did he even know his own heart?

It took me longer to reconcile my Dad's death too. I regretted not being there as much as I could have been. My false sense of guilt and remorse were roadblocks—deterrents on my grief journey. *I should have gone up to him earlier that week when he was still conscious. I talked to him on the phone and knew his end was near. Why didn't I go then? The "shoulds," the "what ifs" can make me crazy with guilt.* I made it to his bedside hours before he passed. He waited for me. I held his hand. Told him I loved him as we surrounded him with love and comfort while he crossed over.

I didn't talk about death and dying with Jon or my father. They wanted to live longer, to focus on getting well and avoided discussing the truth of their situations. They chose denial over what was actually happening.

For several years, we couldn't call Jon's disease "cancer" in front of him and Lisa. Instead, they referred to his brain tumors as blockages and believed in "word voodoo," as if naming it would make it more real. I know this is a choice, a coping mechanism— to avoid the pain of what is and a way to dismiss death and dying.

But I wonder, is this productive and helpful to the person dying and the people close to them?

How can we feel complete with a person? What do we need to do? There's a direct correlation between completing things and how grief and death get processed through us. Discussing death and dying has been key to my grief journey. I would ask anyone grappling with a dying loved one those very same questions. *"What do you need to say and what do you need to do to feel complete with them?"* Sometimes it may be nothing more than being present with them, holding space, as a witness to their passing. Or making amends and taking responsibility for your side of the street in all your affairs with them. Or it's a feeling that occurs when there is authentic transparency and truth with that person in the relationship: that nothing more needs to be spoken of, attended to or processed. And above all, there is respect and acceptance in matters of choice.

In 1995 I attended The Art of Dying Institute's conference and was illuminated through the teachings, lectures and workshops by experts in the Thanatology field (David Kessler, Stephen Jenkinson, Olivia Bareham, Anthony Bossis, Jeanne Denney, Alberto Villoldo…). One question we explored in depth over the weekend was: *"How does living with an awareness of the reality and inevitability of death enhance our ability to live full lives?"*

…Once the clean-up began, following 9/11, a friend and I spent days standing at "Point Thank You" on the West Side Highway, rightly named "Hero Highway," cheering and applauding the thousands of volunteer rescue and recovery workers traveling to the ruins at Ground Zero. It offered me an outlet, a way to feel useful and helpful to the recovery effort by expressing gratitude and support. In the face of this horrific tragedy, I felt vitally alive and connected to the innate goodness and hope of humanity…

Life is fleeting. Take nothing for granted.

Enormous relief washes over me, believing and trusting that my mother, father and brother are together in a better place full of love and peace and forgiveness. And I've moved to a place of tranquil acceptance, hermetic, in the best sense of the word, alone, detached, parentless. Let's face it, after all, at some point in time we all become orphans.

39

THE TRUST

"I'm still upset over the fact that Nicki couldn't stay here. And I have a lot of questions about the Trust. It's so convoluted and poorly written I can't make sense of it," Jan spewed at breakfast.

"Joe's coming over for lunch tomorrow so let's sit down and go over the Trust again with him," I suggested, trying to focus on solutions. "See if we can clear things up."

The following day we sat around eating leftovers from the party for lunch. A pleasant surprise—Ryan showed up. He was on his lunch break and stopped by to visit us, having missed the party and Christmas dinner because he was sick.

I love this. Having a place where family can feel free and comfortable to drop by unexpectedly. We can gather around the large kitchen table and chat, put a pot of coffee on, or pull out food and drinks and serve up a meal on the spot. *Thanks again Mom.*

Ryan calls the condo—The Convention Center.

After sampling all the leftovers, reminiscing and telling party stories and catching up with Ryan, he left to go back to work. Joe, Jan, Bruno and I sat at the table. Bruno wandered off to the living room and Jan and Joe continued small talk. I sensed no one was going to bring up the Trust discussion, so I broached the subject, pulled out my copy of it and Jan opened her digital copy on her laptop. I sat between the two of them bracing myself for any conflict that could ensue.

We went over various sticking points in the Trust, reading through together those few paragraphs about renting the condo and it was clear Joe was trying to remember the lawyer's explanation and decipher her confusing legalese as well.

Jan's voice was tight and rising and she kept interrupting Joe. "This makes no sense. Why is it ok to rent out to a stranger but not to Nicki. She's family for Chrissakes!" Also reacting defensively on the disparity of distributions in the will, "How could a mother do this to her children? You both don't have kids so you can't understand how hurtful this is!"

I felt my face hot and red as I gently placed a hand on Joe's shoulder and tried to mediate.

"Joe, I felt bad too that Nicki couldn't stay here, and I think the wording in this Trust needs to be clarified. Maybe we could make a list of our questions for the lawyer and all sit down with her together to explain it."

Joe agreed wholeheartedly and clearly felt bad about it. He wasn't trying to hurt anyone, least of all Nicki or Jan, only doing his best to follow "the law" and honor Mom's wishes. We would make an appointment to see the lawyer together when I come back up to Maine in February.

…I am committed to the possibility of being a bold articulate communicator committed to love and connection—the mission statement I created for myself in a Landmark Education Communications course years ago. I'm being challenged now to act on my word…

Tudor, the lawyer, was warm, inviting and professional. She ushered us all into her office conference room and even though only Joe was officially her client, as executor of Mom's will, she explained everything in detail to my sister and me as well, clarifying what we were beholden to follow in the Trust and what we could be flexible with, such as to whom and how we rented the condo. And no, there was no "Trust police" making sure we followed certain specific requests in the will. Absolutely we could let Nicki stay there!

Thank God! Enormous relief washed over all of us, particularly Joe. My Mom placed a huge burden on him with her demands and convoluted wording in the will and he was only trying to do his best, make sense of it and follow her dying wishes.

Breakdowns in communication can cause years of unnecessary suffering. When my grandfather died, his gold pocket watch was promised to my mother, but it ended up in the possession of her brother. They didn't speak for fifteen years over this misunderstanding.

Because of my sister's difficulties with my mother, she held back from sharing personal details about her life and her children's, so my mother conjectured, assumed and formulated her own opinions as fact. She had no source of information to lead her to believe otherwise.

"Nicki gives her mother a hard time and treats her terribly," she would say to me. *Sounds like projection to me.* "I email her and she never responds. I've tried calling her and she never returns my calls."

"Mom, you're wrong. Nicki is lovely, kind and considerate," I couldn't begin to unravel the mother daughter dynamics of those two nor was it my place to share any of what I knew. But because Jan didn't share anything, my mother assumed her unhappiness was all about Nicki and she made up a story and blamed her for Jan's sorrows. Or maybe it was a way she could come to terms with her own difficult relationship with Jan and not take responsibility for her part in their dynamic.

Without clear and direct communication, beliefs get misconstrued, narratives formulate and are mistaken for truths.

"Go visit your grandparents," my mother would insist on me every week.

She didn't visit them. Why did I have to? I thought as I'd reluctantly drive over to their apartment on Sundays. I was 20 years old and had much more important things to do than visit my elderly grandparents.

Because Jan's relationship with our mother was fraught with distrust and pain, she didn't encourage her children to continue a relationship with their grandmother on their own. Gregg lived around the corner from her, and she hadn't met his new baby, Charlie, yet. I forwarded pictures of Charlie to my Mom through email. At her age she was still computer literate.

"I can't get my printer to print out a picture of Charlie. I'd love to have one of him. He's adorable and looks just like his mother," she'd say.

I was angry at Jan for denying our mother the pleasure of a great-grandson, so I intervened and texted Gregg and Kate, "why don't they bring Charlie over to meet her. It's her 94th birthday."

"Great idea," Kate responded and they brought flowers, bakery goodies and sweet Charlie over to meet his great-grandmother.

I wonder if severing a relationship with someone in life, without immersing oneself in emotional healing work, in order to make peace with that decision, keeps us haunted and handcuffed to them in death? Does the psyche need to repair and heal these splits to feel complete?

40

FINDING A NEW WAY

Once back in New York City, my brother Joe and I began an email correspondence. He's old school. Doesn't text. So, I've been checking in with him, sharing about our life here in New York and asking him about his.

"…And thx for staying in touch. Email works, right? It's better for me than phone calling," I wrote. "I've never been a phone person."

"I like emails. Also easier to talk for me," Joe wrote back. "…I love you too Joanne and Bruno and look forward for all of us to be together soon. Jan too."

It's nice. I get a rush when I open my inbox and see an email from him. Reminds me of my letter exchange with my Dad when I was away at college. *Damn, I wish I had saved those letters…* I think I'll save my email exchanges with Joe. Like I saved all my text exchanges with Jon. I've even got Jan on board now with a three-way email check in correspondence.

41

THE FINAL CHAPTER

I believe my brother Jon got sick so we could get well but I'm sorry he was the sacrificial lamb for shifting the family dysfunction to a healthier dynamic. Being the glue that kept us together, he pioneered his way; forging and adopting new methods of interacting, courageous in his need and ability to detach completely from my mother which was an impossibility much earlier. He was convinced he had to, in order to survive, and he went on to live for another 46 months with his illness—an outlier, maybe because of it.

Painfully, he chose to separate from us as well. A choice he believed was emotionally healthy. His rationale perplexes me— Did he really want that? Or did he make that decision because of my mother?

"I love Mom and forgive her completely. I feel no animosity towards her anymore. I just can't engage with her at all." He remained clear and definitive.

Perhaps he felt a need to protect her feelings as a last residue of his love and loyalty to her, so she wouldn't feel excluded, and in return admonish us for being neglected? Or was it because of what Lisa needed? Or were they HIS true needs? COVID helped validate his choices, a viable excuse to isolate because of his compromised immune system.

When my Epstein-Barr syndrome gets activated, I have absolute zero energy for anyone but myself. I'm physically and emotionally depleted and tend to withdraw, isolate, avoid people, phone calls, emails and texts from concerned family and friends because it's overwhelmingly exhausting to even respond, or feel the need to update folks on my condition. It's not personal but people tend to take it personally and don't understand (when I don't give them a "thumbs up" response on a text.) EBV is an autoimmune disorder. Unlike cancer, it's not terminal, yet the fatigue symptoms are similar.

I get it Jon! When I'm sick, I completely understand what you were experiencing and why you made those decisions to isolate and pull away from us. But when I recover, I get amnesia and forget.

Our family dynamic has changed since his death. We collapsed and dispersed when he passed. It was an inevitable necessity, but we are reuniting now in a healthier more functional way with clearer boundaries and respect for each other.

Jon's illness and his death broke my heart and forever changed me. There's no going back to who I was before. But my brother and I have a continued connection, and I don't want closure but rather, integration, as I carry his loss with me, recognizing and accepting "a whole life includes pain and sorrow as well as joy."

Exploring my grief through writing and inner spiritual work has opened a portal revealing unhealed childhood wounds, leading me to work with a support program and seek recovery from the effects of growing up in a dysfunctional family.

His dying and death unearthed my own issues—my fear of authority figures, my enabling, people pleasing and approval seeking behaviors, losing my identity in the process. An overdeveloped sense of responsibility toward others has been a mechanism of maintaining control and allowed me to persist in my role of fixer and peacekeeper in the family. I wanted to relinquish these responsibilities and duties, but I wasn't able to disengage.

Now I'm learning that letting go of control happens in stages. After all, I'm trying to change an ingrained behavior that took decades to perfect. Former beliefs, interpretations, and learned behaviors, were values imposed on me when I was young and I adopted them as my own beliefs. Sifting through them now, I'm discerning and discovering my true authentic self.

I recognize and allow myself to feel grief at the loss of my true self; it has lain dormant under the guise of love, worry and concern for others. I now see how this empathy stems from a lack of self-love, distrust and deep feelings of abandonment. I didn't want to monopolize attention. *Enough about me, what about you?* I was more adept at focusing on others, but I see now how that conveys a lack of personal boundaries and fosters resentments. "Focusing on others" appears more admirable from an outside vantage.

I wasn't being honest. When I'm overly concerned with others, I'm distrustful of their capabilities and don't give them the dignity to make their own choices without my intervention or help.

I've always believed in an energetic force greater than myself, but I've adapted my relationship to "it"—call it a Higher Power or God. I've changed how I define it and how I pray to this energy source. I used to barter with God in my prayers. Make deals.

"Please God, if you give me this, I promise I'll do that," I prayed. "Please…take me in place of Jon. I beg you."

I tried bargaining with God, "I'm older and I've had a full life. I've lived enough. I'd be okay to die now, and I know Jon isn't ready." I pleaded. "Please take me instead."

In my prayers, I was dictating what I wanted to happen. Trying to control the outcome. Self will run riot. I didn't know any other way to pray—this is how I was taught, but I'm in recovery now.

A new concept and belief for me is—God doesn't worry. My distorted thinking went like this: *worrying meant I was a good and loving person—that I cared about you, therefore, worrying was an expression of my love for you.* My mother was a worrier and that meant she loved me. Now I realize worrying is the opposite of faith and love. Worrying is praying for what you don't want. Why do people say, "be careful" or "have a safe trip?" Projecting and fearing the worst. I'm trying to shift that paradigm with my words. Instead of "what's the worst that could happen?" Why not "what's the best that could happen?"

I can't say I've completely stopped worrying, but now I can investigate what's underneath the worry more specifically.

I've learned to pray for the courage to allow God's will to work through me and others. "To grant me the serenity to accept the things I cannot change." Jon's cancer. Jon's death. I'm now discovering my authenticity and what I value most. It's been a ponderous yet cathartic process feeling the grief of my childhood wounds. The sadness over the time wasted on adhering to an illusion is turbulent. We can't heal what we don't feel and I'm healing.

I thank my brother for illuminating my journey through this. I'm sorry that he got sick so I could get well. He was my spiritual teacher. Was this his purpose here on earth?

His illness and death brought me to my knees. I'm standing up now. My grief has morphed and changed. I felt an enormous sense of relief once Jon passed which was soon replaced with the pain of his absence—the void of him not being on earth, at times, shock and disbelief, dealing and feeling other people's grief, guilt and anger was unbearable. My "loss" (my job/my purpose of healing and saving my brother) left an emptiness which I realized needed to be devoted to healing my OWN losses and childhood traumas, grieving them and healing from feeling. *"The issues are in the tissues."* Grief and trauma get passed down through generations until someone feels it and works with it. There's no substitute. No getting around it. My brother's death was a window granting access to my healing. I have the support of my spiritual program and I'm re-discovering, uncovering and learning to love my authentic self in this process.

My high school class prophecy said: *"Joanne DiMauro will be still."* Being in constant motion was a way for me to avoid my own demons and pain. A way to remain emotionally intoxicated to protect my vulnerable self. Overachievement—A straight A student followed by a successful career, allowed me to operate above suspicion.

One day in a New York City acting class my anger exploded in an improv exercise. It was the tip of the iceberg. I began to delve into my own emotional healing when the Method acting teacher suggested, "You need to find a place to release your repressed anger." I did and it was the beginning of a tumultuous ride seeking emotional sobriety, with many plummets along the way.

Sometimes we heed the call. A gentle nudge, perhaps; or, unfortunately, instances of getting whacked solemnly with a dose of reality before we make changes.

In 2011, my life was unmanageable: frantically riding my bike up and down town to fitness clients, between my evening health coaching sessions; writing a bi-monthly blog, creating, marketing and facilitating wellness workshops; developing and repurposing audio e-books as products; managing three trainers and a virtual assistant. I was introduced to the Brahma Kumaris, a global spiritual movement, at a peace demonstration in Central Park. I thought to myself, *I really want to start a meditation practice like this, but I just don't have time.*

Be careful what you wish for. I had a shakti-pot moment. While pedaling downtown to a client, completely alone and in my head, going over the massive list of things I needed to accomplish that day, WHAM! I slammed into a car door swinging open and came to a screeching halt, landing hard on the pavement.

In shock, bruised and battered with my hand sliced open like a gutted fish, I was rushed to the hospital. It all happened directly in front of the Brahma Kumaris Center on 5th Ave. A wake-up call for me to stop, reassess my life and slow down. For the next six months I attended meditation classes and learned how to practice stillness. I had no other choice. My body was forced into stillness. Sometimes that's what it takes.

When Jon got sick, I hit a bottom again. I was consumed with anguish, grief and fear and didn't know where to turn for help. I heard a voice inside telling me, *go back to the program*. So, I did. I went back to Al-Anon 12-step program and through the rooms I found ACA, (Adult Children of Alcoholics or Dysfunctional Families), my true home, where I began uncovering and healing my old wounds from the past, and instilling a daily spiritual practice. I embarked on grief educator training through David Kessler's program—turning my pain into purpose.

I now know what emotional sobriety feels like. Not all the time, but I can breathe in the spaciousness of it and recognize it, whereas I never could find my way to it before. I couldn't find the stillness until now.

You were the catalyst for the last chapter of my recovery journey, Jon, and I thank you. How I wished I could have helped and saved you, but I understand now you were way ahead of me. Way ahead of all of us. You were already operating on a different plane of consciousness; in the peace and stillness I'm beginning to appreciate after searching for it for 69 years. I realize you had found your stillness and contentment long ago. Maybe you always were in that place and your dis-ease manifested from frustration in trying to help Mom, help Lisa, help us all find that same stillness and comfort in serenity. You were exasperated, "Don't you get it? Don't you see what really matters?"

I walk through the park on my way home from clients and stop to watch and visit awhile with the hawk who perches high up on the branch of a tree. "Birds of prey are so cool." I hear you saying. I think of you and how you would take the time to appreciate him too.

I don't need to be constantly moving. I am finding happiness in the joy of the present moment. In the quiet and the stillness of just being. You knew and experienced that long before me, Jon. You didn't need my saving.

JON FRANCIS DIMAURO

(written by Lisa Bess)

Jon Francis DiMauro died peacefully on Aug. 31, 2022, at Gosnell House with his devoted wife Lisa Bess by his side. He was born April 30, 1960, and raised in South Portland.

Jon possessed a presence, a quiet elegance unlike anyone anywhere. His stunning blue-green eyes spoke out, searching and kind, filled with thoughts and humor, as though he'd contemplated and fully enjoyed 1000 years seeing through them. Because he was trustworthy, people sought out his good opinion. He was a great listener with highly tuned ears. He was attentive and thoughtful, an easy-going spirit who weighed his words carefully before speaking.

As a carpenter and a contractor, Jon declared himself twice over to be the luckiest guy in the world. He woke each morning grinning enthusiastic about the day ahead. Even better, he worked with his best friend—his brother Joe. He always spoke of an undeniable flow, a harmony they shared which often allowed them to accomplish the work of three men in one day. The brothers also shared a love of sailing the Virgin Islands where they believed the ocean to be a powerful, healing medicine for the body, spirit and soul.

Jon adored his sisters Jan and Joanne. He and Jan shared a side-splitting humor and he raved about her spot-on impersonation of Cher. He felt a kinship with Joanne whose tender, sweet soul mirrored his own and took pride in describing her success as a New York City Rockette. Additionally, Jon admired and cherished his niece, Nicki and his two nephews, Ryan and Gregg. Jon's love of Italian culture was monumental, and no family gathering was complete without his mother Gloria's breaded, pan-fried zucchini or holiday pizzelles.

Beyond family, the voice of nature called out to Jon. In response, he built a remote waterfront camp Downeast. There, he could be alone, play his ukulele, build shorefront blazes, go days without speaking and still crave more silence. Solitude was his heaven on earth. To be perfectly at ease, eyes closed, listening to the birds in the trees suited him. He preferred binoculars over a phone. He was a gentle, contemplative soul who could whistle, imitating many birds, successfully calling them in. Baffling the songbirds gave him a quirky pleasure.

Like his father, Jon had a lifelong passion for golf, blooming onions, and all-you-can-eat buffets. He was a dew sweeper at Riverside and loved every minute on the course. Collecting lost balls from the gully and stream lit him up. He redistributed the balls to other golfers knowing everybody enjoyed saving a few bucks. Jon's natural grace and athleticism extended into absolutely any sport including skiing and karate. He loved basketball, baseball and soccer and was awarded athlete of the year in high school. If on the sidelines, he'd yell his lungs out to cheer on his teammates.

Jon's inner peace was his true gold—his favorite treasure. He valued being told the truth. Operating a good attitude meant everything to him. He often said, "Control your mind. Control your world." He meant it and had little understanding for those who lived bitter, upset, or offended. He'd say, "Life's too short. Don't let anyone steal your peace." Jon lived advocating to choose peace in any circumstance. He particularly embraced these beliefs when he became ill.

With his beloved wife Lisa by his side, Jon spent his last 46 months courageously determined to live well despite facing severe physical disabilities, many surgeries, difficult treatments and a stream of tough diagnoses related to brain and throat cancer. He was committed to beat the odds, to become an outlier, and he did. He lived into the less than 2 percent category.

All throughout, Jon never quit smiling, joking, hoping, or trying his best. Doctors doubted he'd leave his wheelchair, but his dedication to rigorous PT won him enough mobility to drive, which he loved. He focused on what he could do, not the 10,000 things he couldn't. If he woke up, he called the day a gift! Most good days he and Lisa played Scrabble while sipping their morning coffee. His sensitivity, wit, wisdom, connection to spirit, and truthful, authentic lifestyle shone warm as the sun. His attitude amazed people.

Jon was continuously awestruck by the stellar level of medical and emotional care he received from day one. The kindness he sensed at every checkup, treatment, surgery, scan, infusion, transport or ZOOM astounded him. He felt privileged. He had epic appreciation for everyone. To attempt to name out the legion of beautiful souls engaged in Jon's health journey is impossible. Jon believed that anyone working in any aspect of healthcare or emergency services deserves love, warmth and all the respect in the world.

From the start of his illness, Jon and Lisa were an inseparable team. All along they were best friends and each other's everything. Jon was grateful for the loving support and care that Lisa gave to him day-in-and-day-out never leaving his side.

More than 21 years together would have been beautiful, but Lisa and Jon concentrated on the time they did have which was magnificent.

Jon was predeceased by his father, Joseph DiMauro Sr.

Jon is survived by his beloved wife, Lisa Bess; his mother, Gloria C. DiMauro; his brother, Joseph DiMauro Jr. and wife Ursula, his sisters Joanne DiMauro and husband Bruno Iannone, Jan DiMauro; niece Nicole Woods, his nephews, Gregg Woods, Ryan Farr and partner Janet Keith; and his cousins Joseph and Vanessa Capelluti and family; Judith and Jerry McConnell and family; Donald, Richard, Susan, Cindy, Robert, George, Lisa DiMauro and families; Angela, Ann Marie and Joseph Dominicus.

In lieu of flowers, please make donations to:
The Marie Joseph Spiritual Center
10 Evans Rd.
Biddeford, ME 04005
207-284-5671

REFERENCES

Adult Children of Alcoholics/Dysfunctional Families. ACA Fellowship Text (*The Big Red Book*). ACA World Service Organizations, Inc. Lakewood, CA 2006.

Beattie, Melody. *Codependent No More*. Harper Collins, New York 1987.

Bergen, Rev. William. *Unanswered Questions*. St. Ignatius Loyola New York. 2/11/2024.

Bess, Lisa. *Obituary for Jon Francis DiMauro*, Portland Press Herald, Portland, ME, 2022. https://www.pressherald.com/2022/09/11/obituaryjon-francis-dimauro/

Blanton, Madalina at www.soultoearthhealing.com.

Bobbitt, Monica. *A Goat Rodeo*. https://www.facebook.com/agoatrodeo/

Dass, Ram. *You're Not a Wave You're Water*. https://spiritualsoulcenter.org/2024/05/06/six-words/

Fries, James. (1980). "Aging Natural Death, and the Compression of Morbidity." *New England Journal of Medicine*. 303

Greyson, Bruce, M.D. *After*. St. Martin's Publishing Group, New York 2021.

Hahnemann, Samuel. *Organon of Medicine*. B. Jain Publishers, New Delhi 2014.

Iannone, Bruno. "Where You Sing Your Love"

Jenkinson, Stephen. *Die Wise*. North Atlantic Books, Berkeley, CA 2015.

Kessler, David at https://www.Grief.com

Kubler-Ross, Elisabeth & Kessler, David. *Life Lessons*. Scribner, New York 2000.

Pollan, Michael. *Food Rules*. Penguin Books, New York 2009.

Sarno, John, M.D. *The Mindbody Prescription*. Warner Books, New York 1998.

Simms, Meliors. *The Secret Life of Teeth: Understanding Emotional Influences on Oral Health*. Holistic Tooth Fairy Ltd, 2023.

Singer, Michael. *The Untethered Soul*. New Harbinger Publications, Oakland, CA 2007.

Trenkle, Peeka at https://www.PeekaTrenkle.com.

Turner, Kelly A. Ph.D. *Radical Remission Surviving Cancer Against All Odds*, Harper Collin, New York 2014.

Van der Kolk, M.D. *The Body Keeps the Score*. Penguin Books, New York 2014.

ACKNOWLEDGEMENTS

Thank you to James B. Nicola and my fellow colleagues at The NYC International Writers Circle for your on-going support and encouragement of my writing.

Thank you, Catharine Clarke, my creative book producer/editor for walking back into my life at this precious time and guiding me every step of the way to bring my book to fruition. I am deeply grateful to you for all your brilliance, your help, and for your generous open heart. You communicated to your design team what I was feeling, and you "see" me in a way no other publisher would. I thank you for offering me a collaboration working with your team—Erin, on the book cover, and the talented creatives at The Turning Mill in Palenville, New York. A special shout out to Keith Huser for his vibrant cover photo which evokes exactly what I had dreamed of.

I appreciate my friend and talented writer Bill Fitzhugh who generously and gently offered suggestions and critiques along the way and for all my friends who took the time to be readers and gave me thoughtful constructive criticism, comments and feedback.

A special thank you to Elaine Waldman, Adultchildren.org, Stephen Jenkinson and David Kessler who first opened my eyes, and then taught me the skill of grief. I continue to learn. And to all my healers and fellow travelers—without you as my witnesses there would be no healing.

Most of all, I want to thank my loving and talented husband, creative partner in life, Bruno Iannone. You are a master of language, and I am forever grateful for your unwavering support, continued belief in my writing and constant encouragement as well as your astute editing, advice and thought-provoking suggestions. I love you dearly.

All my love to my family. You are my history, my roots and without you there would be no story: to Mom, Dad and most of all to you, Jon. You are loved and missed every day. I dedicate this story to you as a testament of my love.

Joanne DiMauro, Author, Grief Educator, Health Coach, Medical Fitness Specialist, Reiki Master, Novice Homeopath and Herbalist has written and recorded *Know Your Body's Healthy Life Series* of nutrition audio/e-books, a monthly health newsletter and blog, and contributed content to various health/wellness sites, *WorkLife Matters & ME Women Magazine*. Excerpts from her grief memoir, *What Remains Is Love: My Journey of Losing My Brother and Healing through Grief* were published in Kent State's literary journal, *The Listening Eye Magazine*, 2024-25 issue. Highlights of her performing arts career include: Radio City Music Hall Rockette, Bob Fosse Dancer in 1st National Tour of *Sweet Charity*, Greek chorus member in Woody Allen's film, *Mighty Aphrodite*. Performing arts led her to the healing arts.

For the past 28 years, Joanne has operated her own wellness business, offering wellness lectures to organizations as well as nutrition counseling and lifestyle coaching, detox and cooking classes to groups and individuals. She also provides private personal fitness training, incorporating all her healing modalities—Reiki, Medical Fitness & Grief Education—to bring health and wellness to her clients.

www.joannedimauro.com.